THE UNBELIEVABLE TRUTH

JON NAISMITH *and* **GRAEME GARDEN**

Research by BETHAN BIDE

Additional research and verifications by
STEWART McCARTNEY

THE UNBELIEVABLE TRUTH

INTRODUCED BY
MR. DAVID MITCHELL

CONTENTS

INTRODUCTION

PEOPLE, IN GENERAL, tell the truth. That's how society functions. I remember a craze in the playground at school for telling each other things that weren't true. When the person in receipt of the unsolicited lie would respond by saying 'My God!' or 'That's interesting' or even 'Oh', the lie-teller would crow with glee and cry: 'Oh, gullible! You're so gullible! You're a fool to believe that!'

The best way of countering that, I only now realise, would have been to say 'Oh, gullible! I can't believe you believed I believed you!' But, on the several occasions when I was caught out by this scam (before I realised that, until the craze passed, I'd have to affect a perpetual air of incredulity), it would always make me feel angry, but never stupid. It's not fair, I reasoned. How was I supposed to know whether what I was being told was true or not? The lie's very unlikelihood was the ostensible reason for its being worth the time in telling.

And also, I'd impotently think, we're at school. We spend all day every day being told things we didn't previously know and taking them on trust. This is not an appropriate environment for world-weary scepticism. The syllabus would just take far too long to get through if every fact our teachers attempted to impart were met with disbelief.

'You're not getting me with that, sir! Do you expect me to believe that the people of France have completely different words for everything?' 'Copper sulphate, you say? That sounds a bit made-up. I've come across a lot of substances in my life: cheese, soil, cornflakes, poo. This doesn't sound like any of them.' The pull-the-other-one-it's-got-bells-on approach to learning is joyless and time-consuming.

And so it is with life. Human society functions on truth and honesty. The main reason our houses aren't all burgled every day isn't our locks and alarms or the efforts of the police – they only deter a dishonest minority. It's that most of us are disinclined to steal most of the time. We have a civilisation primarily because people are civilised.

Indeed, one of the key human skills which gives us the edge over larger, stronger and more bitey organisms is language – and, beyond that, writing, printing, broadcasting, blogging. Our communication methods are much more effective than a squirt of territory-marking dog's piss or a bee's-hive-informing nectar location dance. We can immediately spread more complicated information: there are delicious mammoths over that hill; plague has reached the neighbouring village; footage of a celebrity giving a blow-job is available by clicking here. But, as a species, we lose that evolutionary edge if we can believe nothing that we're told. If we all have to independently verify every fact we are presented with, the value of our ability to mutually inform is vastly reduced.

I suppose what I'm trying to say, in a roundabout way, is that *The Unbelievable Truth* is a disgrace. It's properly evil. Like parking in a disabled space or not finishing a course of antibiotics. In the name of comedy and entertainment, homo sapiens' evolutionary advantage is being gradually undermined by dozens of episodes consisting of likely-sounding rubbish interspersed with accurate information rendered implausible.

The context in which the programme is broadcast exacerbates the crime: Radio 4, the old Home Service; the most respected network from the greatest public-service broadcaster in the world; the station which burbles constantly in the kitchens of the great and the good. We'll never know the harm that's been done – the half-heard nonsense that's been half-remembered as fact by a captain of industry, flitting from garden to sitting room, which might have led to disastrous misinvestments, lay-offs, despair, suicide. The interesting and unlikely truth which an eminent scientist might have continued to assume was nonsense because his microwave pinged at exactly the moment a panellist buzzed, leading to research avenues prematurely closed off. The damage is incalculable.

The Unbelievable Truth takes lies and puts them in a respectable setting, just like Agatha Christie did with murders. If you've ever been lied to in real life – by a lover, friend, business associate, politician or someone selling you PPI – you'll find it pretty hard to see the funny side, just as very few people enjoy an episode of *Poirot* if they've ever been murdered.

So this book is a repentance. A partial reparation for the programme's crimes. Here, at last, the lying stops (apart from a few regrettable sections written by Graeme Garden – but he's both a comedian and a doctor and you only have to open a newspaper to see what a potent cocktail of self-serving pocket-lining mendacity that must make him). Otherwise, the unbelievable truths have sloughed off their surrounding plausible lies and stand alone: reliable, interesting, funny and odd – like a classic line-up of the show's panellists.

I hope you enjoy this book – and I hope you can forgive us all.

Yours truly,

David Mitchell

ADMIRAL LORD NELSON

Nelson never wore an eye-patch.

He didn't wear anything at all over his damaged right eye, and there is no contemporary portrait of Nelson wearing an eye-patch. Nelson's column in Trafalgar Square shows him without an eye-patch.

Nelson never overcame his seasickness.

Nelson was a sickly person, and it is thought that he was left with incurable sea sickness and recurrent partial paralysis following a bout of malaria whilst on a voyage to India.

Nelson's body was transported home from the Battle of Trafalgar in a barrel of brandy.

Rather than the usual burial at sea, William Beatty, the surgeon aboard the HMS *Victory*, opted to preserve Nelson's remains for the trip back to England as he suspected a state funeral would be ordered for the respected commander. However, when the ship arrived home, Beatty was criticised for failing to keep the body in rum, which was believed to be a better preservative. Legend has it that during the voyage the crew drilled a hole in the barrel and would draw off a little brandy to drink to their hero, hence the term used to describe a sneaky drink: 'Tapping the Admiral'.

Contrary to popular belief, Nelson's last words were 'Drink, drink. Fan, fan. Rub, Rub.'

After being shot by a French sniper, the mortally wounded Admiral repeated the phrase throughout his last minutes whenever he needed a drink of lemonade, cool air, or the ship's chaplain, Dr Scott, to massage his chest.

Had a Yorkshire parson not changed his name to Brontë in honour of Lord Nelson, his famous writer daughters would have been Charlotte, Emily and Anne Brunty.

Patrick Brunty was a huge admirer of Nelson, and changed his name after the King of Naples created Nelson the Duke of Brontë in order to show his gratitude to Nelson after the victory at the Battle of the Nile in 1789. This allowed Nelson to sign himself 'Nelson and Bronte', a title he held dear and used when signing every document he wrote.

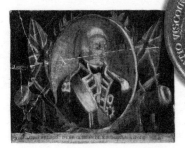

ADOLF HITLER

Hitler and General Franco both only had one testicle.

Nazi medic Dr Johan Jambor, who treated Hitler at the Battle of the Somme, confirmed Hitler had lost a testicle. He said Hitler had asked him if this meant he would still be able to have children. General Franco's doctor's grand-daughter confirmed that Franco had also lost a testicle in battle after an injury to the lower abdomen in 1916. Napoleon is also rumoured to have had one testicle, though it would appear from his autopsy that this was not the case. However, his genitals were reported to have been 'strikingly small, infantile and undersized', the organ in question measuring just $1^1/_4$ inches.

Hitler was *Time* magazine's Man of the Year in 1938.

The honour was also given to Joseph Stalin in 1939 and again in 1942, and to the Ayatollah Khomeini in 1979. Hitler also appeared on the cover of *Time* magazine in 1931, 1933, 1936, 1941 and 1945.

When Adolf Hitler was in power in Germany, it was illegal for any domesticated animal to be called 'Adolf'.

This decree was contained in a 1943 edict issued by Heinrich Himmler, commander of the SS, intended to combat anti-Nazi humour. There was a profound suspicion of the weapon of humour in Nazi Germany. The legal code of the time reflected Joseph Goebbels' description of the political joke as 'a remnant of liberalism' that threatened the Nazi state. Not only was joke-telling made illegal, but those who told jokes were labeled 'asocial' – a segment of society frequently sent to concentration camps. Hitler's second-in-command, Hermann Goering, referred to anti-Nazi humour as 'an act against the will of the Fuehrer. . . and against the State and the Nazi Government', and the crime was punishable by death. A Nazi prosecutor revealed that he determined the severity of the punishment for a joke based on the following theory: 'The better the joke, the more dangerous its effect, therefore, the greater punishment.'

Hitler stipulated that any female character in a German film who broke up a marriage must die before the closing credits.

Before the war, Hitler was extremely interested in cinema and is reported to have seen every film released in Germany. After the Nazi party came to power, when the censors were in disagreement about a film, it was Hitler who made the final judgment. Under Goebbels as Minister of Propaganda, the German film industry was very tightly controlled; Goebbels himself scrupulously checked every one of the 1,363 films released during the 12 years of the Third Reich for any idea that might conflict with Nazi ideology. The 1931 film *Tarzan of the Apes* was banned as it ran contrary to the Nazi ideology of 'hereditary biology'. So strong was the control that it remained long after the end of the Third Reich. In 1965, when *The Sound of Music* opened at the City Palast in Munich, one third of it was missing.

Adolf Hitler's sister-in-law, Bridget Hitler, worked for the British War Relief during the Second World War.

Bridget Hitler, the Irish-born wife of Hitler's older half-brother, Alois, worked for the British War Relief in New York City. In her book *My Brother-in-Law Adolf*, she claimed that it was she who first advised him to trim the edges of his moustache. Her son William Patrick Hitler wrote an article for the American *Look* magazine entitled 'Why I Hate My Uncle'. His Uncle Adolf in turn described him as 'my loathsome nephew'.

ADVERTISING

Elvis Costello's dad wrote and performed the original song 'I'm a Secret Lemonade Drinker' on the ad for R White's in 1973.

Ross McManus's son Elvis Costello, then Declan McManus, played drums and sang backing vocals on the recording. The commercials ran for a remarkable 10 years and in 2007 came 7th in a poll of the national top 100 adverts.

The phrase 'Always a bridesmaid, but never a bride' comes from an advert for Listerine mouthwash.

The advert first featured in the *Ladies' Home Journal* in 1924, with the slogan appearing next to a picture of a forlorn woman called Edna, who was unable to find love because of her bad breath. Listerine was originally sold as a floor cleaner and cure for gonorrhoea.

When Parker Pen marketed a ballpoint pen in Mexico, it was advertised with the slogan 'It won't leak in your pocket and make you pregnant!'

The ads were supposed to read 'It won't leak in your pocket and embarrass you', but this was poorly translated. In Spanish, '*embarazar*' can either mean 'embarrass' or 'impregnate', but when used as a transitive verb it is understood to mean 'to get a woman pregnant'. The correct way to say 'I'm embarrassed' in Spanish is to say '*tengo vergüenza*', meaning 'I have shame'.

An advertising campaign that wafted the aroma of almond liqueur through the London Underground was dropped because the smell was too similar to cyanide gas.

In 2002, a £1.5 million advertising campaign that wafted the smell of Amaretto through the Tube had to be dropped because the day after it started, the *Sun* newspaper ran an article warning commuters that the Underground was a terrorist target, and to be alert for the smell of dangerous gases, particularly cyanide, which smells of bitter almonds.

Mole Valley District Council advertised a concert by the Budapest Gypsy Symphony Orchestra with the words: 'The only time you want to see 100 gypsies on your doorstep'.

The Surrey council sent out 25,000 brochures advertising the concert at Dorking Halls, and then spent £5,000 responding to complaints about the advert.

Bolton's Job Centre banned a company from advertising for a 'friendly' catering manager, arguing that this would discriminate against 'unfriendly' people.

Other words the Job Centre considered discriminatory were 'motivated' and 'enthusiastic'. After complaints to the Department of Work and Pensions, a spokeswoman said: 'we do have guidelines of not using personality traits in adverts to ensure that there is no discrimination in the process, however, a member of staff may have been a bit over-zealous.'

ANCIENT EGYPTIANS

Ancient Egyptian artists painted men brown and women white.

Ancient Egyptian men are almost universally shown with reddish-brown skin, and women with paler skins, although the colour used by Egyptian artists varies over time. In early representations, women are depicted with pinkish white skin, while later on their skin is often yellowish. Some Egyptologists have attempted to explain this colour variation as the work of the sun: upper class women remained indoors while men were out in the sun, and so a lighter-skinned woman appeared more aristocratic.

The Ancient Egyptians used moulted cobra skins as condoms.

Animal intestines and linen were also used. It would appear they did this not as a means of contraception, but as protection against sexually transmitted diseases and as a ceremonial badge of rank.

In the mummification process, the Ancient Egyptians removed the brain with a special hook inserted up the nose.

The first step in the process was the removal of all internal parts that might decay rapidly. The brain was removed by carefully inserting special hooked instruments up through the nostrils in order to pull out the brain in chunks. It was a delicate operation, one which could easily disfigure the face. The embalmers left only the heart in place, believing it was needed on the journey through the underworld.

European painters used a pigment called 'Mummy Brown' or 'Caput Mortuum' made from ground-up mummies.

The pigment was in use from the 16th to 19th centuries and the mummies were taken from excavated Ancient Egyptian communal tombs. Its use was discontinued in the 19th century when artists became aware of its ingredients.

Many cats in Ancient Egypt wore earrings.

Cats were first domesticated in Ancient Egypt over 6,000 years ago. All of our domestic cats today are descended from Egyptian wild cats. Egyptians loved their cats, and considered them to be protectors of the house. Most cats did not have names but were called 'Ta-Mieuw', or 'The Meower'. Cats were so spoiled in Egypt that some wore jewellery such as earrings and nose rings. The occupants of the house in which a cat died would go into a deep mourning and shave their eyebrows.

ANCIENT GREEKS

The Ancient Greeks used Aspirin.
Aspirin is based on a chemical found in willow bark, which the Greeks were using to cure headaches and fevers from 400 BC. The Greek physician Hippocrates even prescribed tea made from willow bark and leaves for this purpose.

In Ancient Greece, the punishment for an adulterous male was the insertion of a large radish into his rectum.
This is known as 'rhaphanidosis', and was the punishment for adultery in 5th- and 6th-century BC Athens. However, in order to apply the punishment, you had to catch the man in the act of adultery with your own wife, in your own house. Other punishments for the same crime included sodomy by mullet fish, or simply killing the perpetrator on the spot.

The Ancient Greeks awarded celery to their sporting champions.

A crown of wild celery would be awarded to winners at the Nemean Games, whereas victors at the Isthmian Games received a garland of dried celery. At the Pythian Games, winners were given laurel garlands, and at Panathenaic Games the prize was first-class Athenian olive oil.

The Ancient Greeks thought the sky was bronze.

Homer refers to the bronze sky in his writings, and also says that both the sea and sheep are the colour of wine. No word for a colour in Ancient Greek makes sense to most people now – we both see the same things, but we are focusing on different aspects of it.

Most Ancient Greeks were idiots.

In Ancient Greece an 'idiot' was a private citizen or layman.

ANTS

At any one time it's estimated that there are as many as a thousand trillion ants.

It's otherwise known as a quadrillion. Their biomass is approximately equal to the total biomass of the entire human race.

A colony of 350,000 ants has collectively the same size brain as a human.

The human brain contains about 86 billion neurons. An ant brain has about 250,000 neurons, so a colony of 350,000 ants has collectively the same size brain as a human.

Some ants actually care for and 'farm' other insects.

One species is known as 'Farmer Ants' and the insects they farm are aphids. Aphids can't use all the sugar they get from plants, so they excrete 'honeydew', which the ants collect to feed the colony. The ants have been known to bite the wings off the aphids in order to stop them from getting away. Ants will transport aphids from plant to plant and take the eggs into their colony for the winter, and will also defend aphids from insect predators, such as ladybirds, by attacking them in large numbers.

A single mega-colony of ants has colonised much of the world, rivalling humans in the scale of its world domination.

Argentine ants living in vast numbers across Europe, America and Japan belong to the same inter-related colony, and will refuse to fight one another. The colony may be the largest of its type ever known for any insect species. Argentine ants were once native to South America, but people have unintentionally introduced the ants to all continents except Antarctica. In Europe, one vast colony of 600 billion Argentine ants is thought to stretch for 6,000 km along the Mediterranean coast, while another of 90 billion extends over 900 km along the coast of California. A third huge colony of 300 million ants exists on the west coast of Japan. Together they are about as brainy as 2,000 humans.

Alpine ant mounds were once used as compasses.

Some ants build mounds with a longer southern slope to increase solar energy collection. The slopes are so consistently oriented that for centuries they were used as compasses by people in the Alps.

APPLES

In Ancient Greece, tossing an apple was a way of proposing marriage; catching it meant you accepted.

The apple was considered sacred to Aphrodite, the Greek goddess of love. According to an epigram by Plato: 'I throw the apple at you, and if you are willing to love me, take it and share your girlhood with me; but if your thoughts are what I pray they are not, even then take it, and consider how short-lived is beauty.' It was believed that just eating an apple would elicit sexual desire, and it was customary in Ancient Greece to eat apples on your wedding night.

In 1996 Ringo Starr appeared in a Japanese advertisement for apple sauce, as 'Ringo' means 'apple' in Japanese.

Apple sauce in Japanese is '*ringosoosu*'.

Apples are better at waking you up in the morning than caffeine.
Although apples do not contain caffeine, they do have the glucose that fuels your brain and gives you energy.

John Glenn ate the first meal in space when he enjoyed puréed apple sauce squeezed from a tube aboard Friendship 7 in 1962.
He was in fact experimenting as scientists thought food in space would collect in the throat and humans would not be able to swallow.

Apple pips contain cyanide.
They contain amygdalin, a cyanide and sugar compound that becomes hydrogen cyanide when metabolised, the same gas used by the Nazis in Second World War concentration camps. Alan Turing, breaker of the Enigma code, was fascinated by the Snow White story, and is believed to have committed suicide by painting an apple with cyanide and eating it.

ARMADILLOS

When the first armadillo specimen was sent to the Natural History Museum in 1832, the curators thought someone must have shaved a piglet and dressed it in bits of armour. It was only when Charles Darwin examined the specimen himself that they realised it actually was a shaved piglet in bits of armour. The first real live armadillo didn't arrive at the Museum until 10 years later, when unfortunately the curators, not wanting to be caught out twice, tried to peel it.

Armadillo shells have been used to make Aztec hard hats, Peruvian mandolins, Venezuelan pyjama cases and Brazilian footballs.

Heston Blumenthal has been known to serve armadillo steaks in his restaurant. According to Heston, the flavour is very similar to cat.

If an armadillo were the size of a human, its penis would be 4 feet long. And if a female armadillo were the size of a human, she'd probably be a scaffolder.

In the 1980s there were several reports of Bolivian drug barons using the armadillo to smuggle cocaine; up to a kilo of the drug can be packed under the shell of a fully-grown adult male. The scheme only came to light when a Customs Officer peeled the shell off an armadillo, trying to show his mates it was only a shaved piglet in bits of armour.

The armadillo is the carrier of more diseases than any other living mammal. A third of all Americans who suffer from leprosy, gonorrhoea, dysentery, haemorrhoids or the plague, catch it from armadillos.

In June 1940 a fleet of 200 armoured pedalos or 'armadillos' set sail from Bournemouth Pleasure Beach, headed for Dunkirk. Sadly, when this Armadillo Armada got to the beach at Dunkirk they were told by Health and Safety that they couldn't take on extra passengers, so they pedalled back to Bournemouth.

The Screaming Hairy Armadillo is a fearsome monster: it's up to 20 feet long with googly eyes and has a hundred teeth. Luckily it spends most of its life in such a deep sleep that not even being hit with a broom will wake it. On the other hand, the Pink Fairy Armadillo looks like a furry prawn and, in Argentina, is specially bred for Christmas, when it's traditionally placed on top of the Christmas Tree.

Like the platypus, some types of Armadillo have a small beak, which can give you a very nasty peck. Such animals were once referred to as 'peccadillos'.

FACT ☺ : The Pink Fairy Armadillo looks like a furry prawn.

FACT ☺ : The Screaming Hairy Armadillo spends most of its life in such a deep sleep that not even being hit with a broom will wake it.

FACT ☺ : A third of all Americans who suffer from leprosy, catch it from armadillos.

FACT ☺ : If an armadillo were the size of a human, its penis would be 4 feet long.

FACT ☺ : Armadillo shells have been used to make Peruvian mandolins.

ARTHUR CONAN DOYLE

Sir Conan Doyle was a founder and the first goalkeeper of Portsmouth FC.
While living in Southsea and writing his first two Sherlock Holmes stories, Arthur Conan Doyle played football under the pseudonym A.C. Smith. His team, the Portsmouth Association Football Club, later became Portsmouth FC.

It's said that Sir Arthur Conan Doyle helped Italian marathon runner Dorando Pietri over the finish line at the 1908 Olympic games, leading to his disqualification.
He was reporting on the race for the *Daily Mail*, and witnessed Pietri, suffering from heat exhaustion and too much brandy, collapse five times and run the wrong way in the final stages of the race. Arthur Conan Doyle felt so guilty about the disqualification that he helped raise some £300 on his behalf, and Pietri became an international celebrity.

Arthur Conan Doyle and Harry Houdini fell out after Houdini tried to convince Doyle that he did not have supernatural powers.
Houdini contradicted his friend's belief that his spectacular escapes were due to his supernatural powers, and demonstrated

that spiritualist messages could be 'received' through trickery. Unlike his logical creation Holmes, Arthur Conan Doyle believed in the spiritualism popular at the time, and publicly endorsed the fake Cottingley fairies photographs.

Arthur Conan Doyle was awarded his knighthood not for his Sherlock Holmes books but for a pamphlet he issued in defence of the British concentration camps during the Boer Wars.

Although best remembered for his literary work, his honour came as a result of a booklet entitled 'The War in South Africa: Its Cause and Conduct', which defended the British against allegations of participating in rape, torture and the establishment of concentration camps. Doyle had served as a volunteer doctor in a field hospital during the campaign, and wrote the 60,000 word document in only eight days.

Sir Arthur Conan Doyle played cricket for the MCC and once bowled out the legendary W.G. Grace.

However, Conan Doyle's dismissal of Grace was described as his 'only first-class wicket' during the match. Afterwards, Doyle wrote a long poem describing the incident, entitled 'A Reminiscence of Cricket'. This illustration shows Conan Doyle himself losing his wicket, as well as a chunk of his bat.

BANANAS

The banana tree is not actually a tree, but a giant herb.

Although the banana itself is a fruit, containing the seeds of the plant, the tree itself is technically regarded as an herbaceous plant, because the stem does not contain the woody tissue required of fruit trees.

In the Koran, a banana, rather than an apple, is thought to be the forbidden fruit that tempted Eve.

According to the Koran, the banana is the tree of paradise, which is why its scientific name is 'Musa Paradisiaca'. Some horticulturalists believe the banana was the earth's first fruit.

Most banana plants have not had sex for 10,000 years.

Almost every banana we eat is propagated by hand, a process which first started in the jungles of South East Asia at the end of the last ice age. As a result, scientists are worried that the banana lacks the genes to fight off modern-day pests and diseases, and could face extinction.

In 2001, there were more than 300 banana-related accidents in the UK.

Most of these involved people slipping on the skins. In 2012, Sainsbury's announced it had developed non-slip bananas, but sadly this turned out to be an April fool.

Reindeer love bananas.

Although originating from very different natural habitats, reindeer herders report that the animals will seek out the fruit from their pockets.

A bunch of bananas is called 'a hand'.

This collective noun derives from Arabic, where the word 'banan' means finger. As growing bananas naturally divide into clusters, each containing around eight to twenty fruits, these fingers form a hand.

BARBIE

Barbie is modelled on a German sex doll called Lilli.

Lilli was an adult figure doll for men marketed as a 'sexual fantasy figure' and 'blonde bombshell and woman of the world'. Lilli started life as a cartoon strip in the German newspaper *Bild*, and spent her time chatting with girlfriends about fashion and sex, flirting with boyfriends and arguing with her boss. Barbie's manufacturers Mattel acquired the rights to Lilli in 1964, after which production of the Lilli doll ceased.

Early Barbies had nipples.

The first four models, made in 1961 and known by collectors as 'ponytails', had nipples. These disappeared after complaints from parents, with some reports saying that Mattel filed them down before they left the factory.

If a real woman were to have Barbie's proportions, she would have to walk on all fours.

Barbie's legs are 50 per cent longer than her arms, where a normal woman's are only 20 per cent longer. This, combined with her small feet and large bust, would cause her to continually fall forward. Additionally, she would need someone to support her head whilst crawling because her neck is twice as long as the average woman's. Barbie's waistline is so small that her body would have room for only half a liver and a few centimetres of intestine, resulting in her suffering from chronic diarrhoea and death from malabsorption and malnutrition. Barbie would also have a BMI of only 10, meaning she'd fit the weight criteria of an anorexic and would lack the 17 per cent body fat required for a woman to menstruate or conceive.

In 1997, a disabled teenager pointed out that Barbie's wheelchair-bound friend 'Share a Smile Becky' didn't fit into the lift in Barbie's house.

Mattel responded to criticisms by announcing the launch of the new Barbie folding pretty house, with a wider front door and no stairs. Other controversial Barbies include the 1965 'Slumber Party Barbie', which came with a miniature book entitled *How To Lose Weight* with the sole advice: 'don't eat', and 'Teen Talk Barbie', who spoke a number of phrases including 'Will we ever have enough clothes?' and 'Math class is tough', the latter of which drew complaints from the American Association of University Women.

Fruit flies with the 'Ken and Barbie' gene have no external genitalia due to a genetic mutation.

Other mutations in fruit flies include the Tinman, which, like the *Wizard of Oz* character, has no heart, and the Groucho Marx, a fly that produces an excess of facial bristles.

BATS

In the Tyrol it was widely believed that carrying the left eye of a bat in your pocket would make you invisible.

Elsewhere in Austria it was once believed that tying the heart of a bat to your arm with red string would ensure you always won at cards.

In 1943, the US Army developed a new incendiary bomb involving bats with napalm strapped to their wings.

The US military had planned to release the bats over Japanese cities, imagining that when the bats went to roost in the wood and paper buildings, they would go up in flames. Aside from the atomic bomb, another reason for abandoning the project was that on their first airborne test, the bats burned a US army base to the ground.

The bat-bomb canister pictured above was used to house the hibernating bats. It would be dropped from high altitude over the target area attached to a parachute. As it fell, the bats would warm up and awaken, until at 1,000 feet, the bomb would open and release over 1,000 bats, each carrying a tiny time-delayed napalm incendiary device, to roost in flammable wooden Japanese buildings.

The US Army Base in Carsbad, New Mexico was set alight by errant bats from the experimental bat bomb project.

The woolly bat of West Africa lives in spiders' webs.

More than 1,000 colonial spiders may live in one of these large, intricate webs, and the bats can stay well hidden in the cluster of leaves that form the central part of the web.

The greater bulldog bat is an expert fisherman.

The Central and South American bat fishes by raking its large, taloned feet through the water and impaling prey on hooked claws. This method can result in a catch of up to 30 fish in a single trip. The bats get their name from their cheek-pouches, which they use for storing food.

Vampire bats urinate while they are sucking blood.

The bats start urinating whilst feeding in order to get rid of excess water they take in, which could cause them to become too heavy to fly.

B.B.C.

BBC Television used to be shut down completely between 6pm and 7pm to make sure parents put their children to bed.

This was known as 'The Toddlers' Truce', and lasted until 1957, when ITV broke the agreement by filling the slot with filmed adventure serials.

In 1966, an episode of children's show 'Pinky and Perky' was banned for being too political.

The episode was entitled 'You Too Can Be Prime Minister', but was banned as the BBC were fearful of political content in the run up to a general election. However, public outcry saw it reinstated, and the episode went on to attract more viewers than Harold Wilson's party political broadcast, which was showing at the same time over on ITV. During the same election campaign, Harold Wilson successfully lobbied the BBC to have *Steptoe and Son* rescheduled, fearing it would interfere with the Labour party election turnout.

When Radio 4's *Woman's Hour* first aired in 1946, it had a male host.

The first presenter was Alan Ivimey, and the programme was initially scheduled at 2pm; a time when morning domestic chores and lunchtime washing up were done, but before the children came home from

school. Early items included 'How to hang your husband's suit' as well as the more adventurous sounding 'Cooking with whale meat' and 'I married a lion tamer'.

During the Cold War, British nuclear submarines were instructed that if the *Today* programme was off-air without explanation for three consecutive days, it was a signal that Britain had been wiped out.

Historian professor Peter Hennessy maintains in his book *The Secret State: Whitehall and the Cold War 1945–1970*, that upon this signal, the commanders of British nuclear submarines were to open sealed instructions from the Prime Minister on how to respond. Hennessy believes that this test still applies to Trident submarines today.

The BBC's *Green Book*, published in 1949, forbade jokes about stammering, chambermaids, weddings, solicitors, the Boer War, and vulgar use of the word 'basket'.

Under guidelines on vulgarity, the book stated:

There is an absolute ban upon the following:-
Jokes about – Lavatories, Effeminacy in men, Immorality of any kind

Suggestive references to – Honeymoon couples, Chambermaids, Fig leaves, Prostitution, Ladies' underwear, e.g. winter draws on, Animal habits, e.g. rabbits, Lodgers, Commercial travellers

Extreme care should be taken in dealing with references to or jokes about –
Pre-natal influences (e.g. 'His mother was frightened by a donkey'), Marital infidelity

Good taste and decency are the obvious governing considerations. The vulgar use of such words as 'basket' must also be avoided.

BEARDS

Cleopatra wore a false beard.

In Ancient Egypt a false beard was worn by queens as well as kings. It was held in place by a ribbon tied over the head and attached to a gold chin strap. Certain types of beard – in particular one that was closely plaited – were strongly associated with divinity. For this reason, pharaohs of either gender would wear a false beard in certain ceremonial situations to emphasise their god-like qualities.

Russia's Peter the Great imposed a beard tax.

He imposed the tax as part of an effort to westernise his nobility – most men in Europe were by then clean shaven. Everyone above the lowest class had to pay 100 roubles for a copper or silver 'beard token', which had a moustache and a beard engraved onto it and the message 'the beard is a useless burden'. Clerks were stationed at the gates of every town to collect the beard tax. Henry VIII and his daughter Queen Elizabeth I had launched a similar tax in the 16th century.

Josephine Clofullia, the most famous bearded lady of all time and a prominent attraction in P. T. Barnum's side show in the 19th century, had a beard six inches long when she was only 16.

Josephine was an ardent admirer of the French monarch Napoleon III, and she styled her beard after his. So sincerely flattered was the ruler when he learned of this imitation that he sent Madame Clofullia a large diamond, which she wore, appropriately, in her beard.

Frederic Chopin wore a beard on only one side of his face, saying that when he performed at the piano the audience only saw one side.

Chopin's beard covered only the right side of his face, in all likelihood because he was unable to grow facial hair properly following a series of illnesses. When he did try to follow the fashion of the time, it grew spasmodically and unevenly, and when he was asked about it, he made the quip about being seen by the audience from one side only.

A man's beard grows fastest when he anticipates sex.

This was confirmed in 1970 by an anonymous Cambridge scientist writing in a letter entitled 'Effects of Sexual Activity on Beard Growth In Men' published in the scientific journal *Nature*. While on a near remote island, he had measured his beard growth 'by collecting and weighing the shavings from the head of a Philips Philishave razor'. He discovered that during the day or so before sexual activity, his beard grew much faster and that, within a day or two of resuming sexual activity, his beard growth slowed.

BEARS

The Romans set polar bears against seals in flooded amphitheatres.

In his eclogues of AD57, Calpurnius Siculus describes the practice during a set of lavish spectacles hosted by Emperor Nero: 'Beast of every kind I saw; here I saw snow-white hares and horned boars, here I saw elk, rare even in the forests which produce it. . . Nor was it my lot only to see monsters of the forest: sea calves [seals] also I beheld with bears pitted against them.'

Henry III kept a polar bear in the Tower of London, and allowed it to go fishing in the Thames.

The bear was a gift from the King of Norway in 1252, and records at the Tower show expenses were claimed for a 'muzzle and an iron chain to hold the bear when out of the water and a long and strong cord to hold it when fishing in the Thames'.

Ivan the Terrible had an Archbishop sewn into a bearskin and hunted down by a pack of hounds.

Ivan admitted that he had condemned Leonidas, Archbishop of Novgorod, to this fate, but claimed he had only acted 'in conformity with fair justice' in doing so.

Lord Byron kept a pet bear in his rooms while a student at Cambridge.

Byron acquired the tame bear in defiance of the university's rules, which forbade anyone from keeping a dog in their rooms, but made no mention of ursine companions. When asked what he meant to do with the bear, Byron suggested, 'he should sit for a fellowship'.

BYRON

HE KEPT A BEAR IN HIS COLLEGE DORM BECAUSE THEY WOULDN'T ALLOW DOGS.

A bear was the first living creature to test a supersonic ejection seat.

The Stanley Aviation company developed the ejector capsule, which would allow a pilot to survive in extreme altitude or speed conditions, and used a live bear as a test subject in 1962.

BEDS

1 in 10 European babies is conceived in an IKEA bed.

Such is the company's dominance, IKEA is now the world's third largest consumer of wood globally. In spite of this, they try to keep their products rooted in their heritage; chairs are usually named after common Swedish men's names, curtains are given Swedish women's names, and garden furniture is named after Swedish islands. As a result, 'Dick', 'Prick' and 'Bugga' are all names that have been considered for production.

In old Hollywood films, no couple were permitted to appear in bed unless both the man and the woman had at least one foot on the floor.

When the Hays Office censored Hollywood films, the regulations suggested this as a method to avoid the taboo of a 'horizontal embrace'. These regulations also stipulated details such as the maximum length of an acceptable kiss.

Hans Christian Andersen died from falling out of bed.

He was hurt after falling out of bed in 1872, and died from the injuries three years later. He was very unlucky; the odds of death by falling out of bed are one in two million.

Charles Dickens slept with his head at the north end of his bed, which was aligned from north to south.

Dickens suffered from insomnia, and found this arrangement helped where opium and alcohol had failed. His daughter reported that he would rearrange the furniture in a room to enable his bed to lie north to south, even if he was only spending one night there, and that he would check he was laying in the exact centre of the mattress by measuring with his arms. Dickens believed this helped as it allowed him to connect with the electrical currents of the earth.

According to recent research, the average bed lasts longer than the average marriage.

The average bed is replaced every 12 years and 5 months whereas the average British marriage lasts for 11 years and six months.

BEER

St Bridget of Kildare was renowned for transforming her used bathwater into beer.

Probably the best-known Irish saint after St Patrick, St Bridget is noted for the miracle of changing her dirty bathwater into beer for visiting clerics. Bridget is also said to have supplied beer out of one barrel to 18 churches, and a poem attributed to her in the Burgundian Library in Brussels begins with the line: 'I should like a great lake of ale for the King of the Kings.'

'The London beer flood' destroyed two houses and killed nine people in 1814.

The incident, which was widely reported in *The Times*, occurred when a huge tank in Tottenham Court Road brewery pictured below ruptured and created a giant wave containing over a million litres of beer, which crashed through the building's 25-foot brick wall. Despite the death and destruction caused, hundreds ran outside with pots and pans to collect the beer, with some stooping to lap it up as it washed through the streets.

Henry VIII decreed that any servant who impregnated a maid had to go without beer for one month.

The court regulation stipulated: 'such pages as cause maids of the king's household to become mothers shall go without beer for a month.'

Carlsberg Special Brew was created for Winston Churchill on the behest of the Danish government.

According to Carlsberg's website: 'Special Brew was originally brewed for Winston Churchill. His visit to Copenhagen in 1950 was commemorated with a "special" brew produced in his honour. . . as Churchill's favourite drink was cognac, the brewers at Carlsberg created a stronger lager with cognac flavours amongst its tasting notes.'

Among the Buganda people of Uganda, widows of a recently deceased king have the honour of drinking the beer in which his entrails have been cleaned.

The people of this ancient kingdom also practice divination by reading the patterns of urine on banana leaves. Unfortunately, some of their ritual sexual practices have been blamed for leaving the people particularly susceptible to AIDS.

BELLS

In medieval times, bells were thought to stop thunderstorms.

It's a widespread belief across the world that the sound of bells scares off evil spirits. Because storms were attributed in Christian belief to Satan, the Lord of Air, church bells would be rung in an attempt to stop them. The inscription 'Fulgura Frango' or 'I break up the lightning flashes' was common on medieval bells. Many bell ringers were killed by lightning as a result, even as late as the 18th century. From 1753 until 1786, lightning struck 386 French church towers, with lightning running down the bell ropes killing 103 French bell ringers. The fact that the local church often had the best cellars in which to store gunpowder didn't help either. In 1769, a lightning bolt struck the tower of St Nazaire in Brescia, where 100 tons of gunpowder was stored. The resulting explosion destroyed one-sixth of the city and killed 3,000 people. As late as 1856, lightning struck the church of St Jean on the island of Rhodes causing the gunpowder in the vaults to explode, and 4,000 were killed.

Under a law of 1888, rather than just using the bell on your bike occasionally to warn people in your path, every single cyclist in Britain was legally required to ring the bell on their bike non-stop.

The 1888 law recognised the bicycle as a 'carriage', and as such allowed it to formally use the roads, providing it had an audible means of warning. The law was abolished in 1930.

Henry Ford's first motor vehicle was fitted with a domestic door-bell instead of a horn.

Ford called his vehicle a 'quadricycle' because it resembled two bicycles held together by a frame. It was powered by a two-cylinder engine and steered by a tiller.

Mary Whitehouse tried to get Chuck Berry's 1972 hit record 'My Ding-a-ling' banned from the BBC on the grounds that it was intended to stimulate self and mutual masturbation.

The BBC rejected her claim; quoting Chuck Berry, they said the record was plainly about a boy who was given a bell to play with. The song went on to become Berry's first UK number one single. As the former *Observer* columnist Tom Hibbert pointed out, this may have been the one supportable crusade of her career.

Bells were used to prevent the Black Death.

Breaking up the air with loud noises was thought to dissolve the 'static plague vapors', so towns rang church bells and held parades where the citizens banged pots and pans in the street. During later outbreaks of plague in the 17th century, cannons and muskets were shot.

BICYCLES

The modern bicycle was invented by a Scottish blacksmith. It was made of wood and its front was carved in the shape of a horse's head.

In 1839, Kirkpatrick MacMillan added pedals to the velocipede, a contraption that was powered by the rider's feet running along the ground.

Before brothers Orville and Wilbur Wright became aircraft pioneers, they ran a bicycle repair business.

After first only repairing bicycles from their cycle shop in Dayton, Ohio, the Wright brothers soon moved into rentals and sales, eventually building their own models. The profits funded their aviation experiments, and they used the shop building to conduct their pioneering wind tunnel tests as well as to build their first aircraft.

The longest bicycle in the world is over 92 feet long.

The bicycle was built by members of Gezelschap Leeghwater, the mechanical engineering students' association at Delft University of Technology, and it was ridden a distance of 100 metres in 2002.

**In the 1908 Olympics, Ireland beat Germany
3–1 at bicycle polo.**

Bicycle polo was popular enough to be a
demonstration event at the games, although
it did not reappear at the 1912 Olympics.

**The European patent office lists nine
devices for tethering a dog to a bicycle in
order to exercise it.**

Devices range from guards that enclose
and protect the dog as it runs alongside the
bicycle to more simple tethers and harnesses.
Some are commercially available.

BOXES

Give the
Grocer a Wink
-and see what you'll get
K-T-C

A 1907 ad campaign for Kellogg's Toasted Corn Flakes offered a free box of cereal to every woman who would wink at her grocer.

The 'Give the Grocer a Wink' campaign invited women to 'wink at your grocer and see what you get'. Kellogg's were early pioneers of cereal promotions, and in 1910 'The Jungleland Funny Moving Pictures Book' became the first of thousands of gifts offered to consumers.

The prudish Victorians invented the 'self-abuse alarm', a small box wired to a buzzer and attached to a young man's penis.

This contraption allowed worried parents to hear a buzzer in the event of nocturnal activity. One cruder method involved spiked rings worn around the penis, and Dr I. Bloch, in *The Sexual Life of Our Time*, writes of doctors 'who appeared before the child armed with great knives and scissors and threatened a painful operation or even to cut off the genital organs' as a preventative method.

Many American shops refused to stock a breakfast cereal, as they believed the pink hippo on the box was gay.

Punch Crunch was a fruit-flavoured cereal, shaped in pink rings, that came in a pink box fronted by Harry the pink hippo. Harry S. Hippo, who wore a sailor suit and had long eyelashes, was retired following accusations about his sexuality from a right-wing media watchdog, who also believed he was trying to hit on Cap'n Crunch.

According to a ROSPA report, cardboard boxes caused 10,492 accidents in 2002.

Cardboard boxes were beaten by tights, which scored an impressive 12,003 injuries, but were ahead of cotton buds, which scored 8,751.

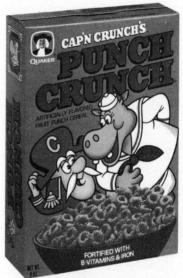

The controversial rock musician Marilyn Manson collects old tin lunchboxes.

He says some of his favourites include his 'Land of the Giants' and his 'Doctor Dolittle' lunchboxes. He's written a song called 'Lunchbox' and smashed someone in the face with one during a fight in a club.

BOY SCOUTS

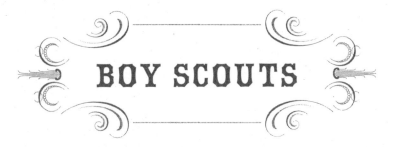

Indonesia has over 17 million scouts.

As of 1 December 2010, the governing body for scouts in Indonesia had 17,103,793 members, more than any other country. This figure includes some members of the World Association of Girl Guides and Girl Scouts, or WAGGGS.

Lord Baden-Powell warned young men to 'keep the organ clean and bathe it in cold water' to fend off the fearsome 'rutting sensations'.

Baden-Powell's 1922 book *Rovering to Success* contains five chapters, each tackling a different 'rock' on which a young man might crash his canoe. These 'rocks' are Horses, Wine, Women, Cuckoos and Irreligion, although Powell points out that all the potential pitfalls really stem from just one cause: 'the rutting season'.

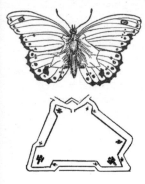

While in the military, Lord Baden-Powell frequently travelled disguised as a butterfly collector.

Baden-Powell acted as a spy during the Boer War, and disguised plans of Boer fortifications and gun emplacements in sketches of butterfly wings, leaves and even an intricate stained-glass window.

The scouts were banned by both Hitler and Stalin.

Most fascist countries and almost every communist country have banned the scouts. Instead the Nazis set up the Hitler Youth, an organisation Baden-Powell was initially keen to form ties with. In a diary entry from 1939, Baden-Powell notes 'lay up all day, read *Mein Kampf*. A wonderful book, with good ideas on education, health, propaganda, organisation etc.'

Paul McCartney missed the debut Cavern Club gig of the Quarrymen, the first incarnation of the band that would become the Beatles, because he was away at scout camp.

The band first played at the famous Liverpool venue in 1957, where, despite instructions from the manager not to play rock and roll, John Lennon played a version of Elvis' 'Don't Be Cruel'.

BRAS

When opinion turned against her in the Philippines, Imelda Marcos wore a bullet-proof bra.

When she fled her people, Mrs Marcos was forced to abandon her bulletproof bras, 1,000 handbags, gallons of perfume, and the designer shoe collection of 3,000 pairs, which she kept in the sprawling Manila palace.

Howard Hughes used his aeronautical engineering knowledge to design the first cantilevered push-up seamless bra for then unknown starlet Jane Russell.

Hughes made it his personal business to make the most of Miss Russell's assets as she lay in the hay in the film *The Outlaw*. Hughes had his engineers design a special 'cantilever' underwire bra with no noticeable seams that would up-lift the contour of the bosom. Russell later said the 'ridiculous' contraption hurt so much that she wore it only a few minutes before secretly slipping back into her old bra. Nevertheless the film's release was delayed for three years because of Russell's sensuous portrayal before Hughes finally decided to release it without a Motion Picture Code seal.

The Japanese invented the ice bra to keep the wearer cool in warm weather.

International lingerie maker Triumph produced what it called the 'Super Cool Bra' in Japan made with refrigerated cooling gel pads. The brassiere could be worn with a skirt made of a mosquito net or bamboo shades, adding to its ability to offer relief in hot weather.

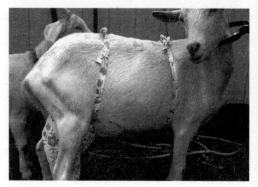

Both versions come with a small hanging wind chime that in Japan is believed to sound refreshing. There is even a little bamboo ladle added for good measure, in case the wearer wants a splash of water.

In 1995, a herd of goats on the Isle of Wight were fitted with bras to protect their udders.

Isle of Wight housewife Iris Chilverton designed goat-sized bras to stop her goats' udders getting snagged by prickly thorns and gorse bushes.

Women in the war years made their own bras from damaged parachutes.

British bra production virtually ground to a halt between 1939 and 1945 as the steel and rubber was needed for the war effort. In the war era after 1940, many women made their own bras from paper patterns or magazine guidelines. The fabric they used was sometimes parachute silk, parachute nylon or old satin wedding dresses.

BREAD

It was once customary to use pieces of bread to erase lead pencil before rubber erasers came into use.

The soft parts of bread can be used to erase lead, chalk, graphite and crayon, as the bread is composed of molecules that are stickier than those of the paper, meaning the marking material becomes stuck to the bread.

German pumpernickel bread derives its name from the German words *nickel* meaning 'devil' and *pumper* meaning 'to break wind'.

The bread was given this name by the Westphalian Germans as the sour rye bread was said to be so difficult to digest it even made Satan break wind. An earlier German name for it was *krankbrot* or 'sick bread'.

A machine to slice bread was invented in 1912, but took 16 years to catch on as bakeries were unimpressed that the machine held cut loafs together with metal hat pins.

Otto Frederick Rohwedder's invention didn't take off until he adapted his machine to also wrap the bread, preventing it from drying out. Sliced bread became commercially available for the first time in 1928, under the name 'Sliced Kleen Maid Bread', and its even slices were handy for the newly invented pop-up toaster.

In 2001, British design student Robin Southgate developed a weather forecasting toaster that would print the day's weather prediction onto toasted bread.

The toaster takes meteorological information from the internet, and an image is burned onto the bread by one of three stencils, representing sunny, cloudy or rainy conditions.

The Museum of Burnt Food in Arlington, Massachusetts, houses some 50,000 specimens of burnt food, including over 2,000 in the Hall of Burnt Toast.

The museum also boasts one wing devoted especially to burnt legumes, some carbonised elephants, and a newly renovated 'hall of charred condiments'. The museum even has its own motto: 'To Cook the Museum Way – always leave the flame on low . . . and then take a long nap.'

BREASTS

The space between a woman's breasts is known as the 'intermammary sulcus'.

On 27 August 1997 the International Federation of Associations of Anatomists officially named the space, as the term cleavage was thought too imprecise.

In the 1890s it was fashionable for women to have their nipples pierced by a jeweller.

After the nipples were pierced, gold 'bosom rings' were inserted, often joined together by a small gold chain. They were thought to enlarge the appearance of the breasts, and keep them in a state of constant excitement. A fashion feature in *The Times* gave this advice on pierced nipples: 'One looks fine and dandy. Two makes you look like a chest of drawers.'

The mermaid on the original Starbucks logo had bare breasts.

It was based on a 17th century Norse woodcut, and depicted a topless siren. In the subsequent versions the breasts have been covered by her flowing hair.

In the 1880s there was a woman who had ten breasts, all of which secreted milk.

A scientist called Neugebauer recorded this incident in 1886. There have been many recorded instances of polymazia throughout history, including a woman with two nipples on a single breast, each of which expressed milk. Often mistaken for moles, supernumerary nipples are common; appearing along two vertical 'milk lines', they are diagnosed at a rate of 1 in 18 humans.

A man in Florida sued a topless club, claiming he had suffered whiplash injuries after a dancer thrust her breasts into his face.

In 1996, Paul Shimkonis alleged he suffered pain, disfigurement, mental anguish and loss of capacity for the enjoyment of life after his encounter with a 60-inch bust on the eve of his wedding. He claims, 'It was like two cement blocks hit me. I've never been right since', to which the manager of the Diamond Dolls club responded by saying, 'If I had been injured, I'd have just loved it. I wouldn't complain'.

CABBAGE

I LIKE DOGS.
BUT NOT THIS BREED

During the First World War, sauerkraut was renamed 'liberty cabbage'.

At this time in the US, any reference to German things was considered unpatriotic. Other changes included 'liberty sandwich' for 'hamburger', and 'liberty measles' for 'German measles'.

Scientists claim that sauerkraut is as effective as Viagra at improving sexual function.

A study at King's College London concluded that pickled cabbage is one of nature's most powerful aphrodisiacs, and suggested that all men eat 'pickled cabbage' twice a day.

The largest cabbage ever recorded was over three times the size of a space hopper and weighed as much as Beyoncé.

The red cabbage was grown by William Collingwood of County Durham in 1865. It had a circumference of 259 inches and weighed 123 pounds. Mr Collingwood also grew very large leeks, his largest reportedly measuring 10 feet 4 inches and having a circumference of 14 inches.

The Roman writer Cato recommended that women should bathe in the urine of a person who habitually ate cabbage.

Cato believed cabbage had such a high medicinal value, that by washing her genitalia in the solution, a woman would never become diseased. He believed that the health-giving properties of cabbage surpassed those of all other vegetables, and that it could be prepared to make an excellent laxative or antiseptic, as well as a cure for indigestion, headaches, eye infections, fevers and a range of other ailments. Cato prescribed the urine of a cabbage eater as 'wholesome for everything', and recommended that babies should be bathed in it. According to his writings, cabbage may be eaten either cooked or raw, but he recommends 'if you eat it raw, dip it into vinegar'.

The Egyptians worshipped cabbage heads as gods and built them elaborate altars.

This is thought to be because they saw symbolic significance in the cabbage's overlapping layers. The Romans also attributed special powers to the cabbage, thinking it held life-giving properties and developing a whole branch of medicine around it, including placing cabbage leaves on wounds and believing that cabbage protected against the effects of alcohol and prevented hangovers.

CAKE

The English word for posh cake is gateau and the French word for posh gateau is 'le cake'.

'*Le cake*' is often a rich fruitcake. The French also eat a savoury starter called 'le cake', which is loaf-shaped and contains bacon, cheese, olives, onions or sausage.

The cake on the sleeve of the Rolling Stones *Let It Bleed* album was baked by TV chef Delia Smith.

Delia was working as a home economist in 1969 when she was commissioned to bake a cake for the photo shoot. She said she'd been told to make it 'very over-the-top and as gaudy as I could'.

In the 19th century, arsenic was often used to create green cake icing.

A green cake decoration sold in Greenock, Scotland, with the inscription 'for the bairnies', contained seven times the fatal adult dose of arsenic, with fatal consequences. Such was the sense of national shock that the experience was to pervade the Scottish attitude to green confectionery well into the 20th century, with the professor of forensic medicine at Glasgow University observing in 1954: 'fewer green sweets are sold in Scotland than in any other country'.

A team of British bakers cooked up a cake in the shape of a full-sized Skoda car using 180 eggs, 125 jars of jam, and 100 kg of sugar.

The car was a Skoda Fabia, and its tyres were made of chocolate icing, the rear lights were jelly, the wipers were liquorice, the headlight covers were glacier mints, the moulded bodywork was a Rice Krispies mixture and the engine was filled with syrup. It was made for a TV advert, which cost £500,000 and took 10 days to make.

***The Satanic Verses* author Salman Rushdie wrote the 'Naughty But Nice' slogan for cream cake adverts.**

Rushdie worked for an advertising agency in the 1970s, during which time he also came up with the 'Think Bubbles' campaign for Aero chocolate, coining the words 'irresistabubble', 'unforgetabubble', 'delectabubble' and 'incredibubble'.

CAMELS

Camel races in the United Arab Emirates have started to feature robot jockeys.

The lightweight robots were reportedly developed by a Swiss company and sell for $5,500 each. They are controlled via a remote control system, and can lean from side to side and pull the reins. The robots take the place of traditional child jockeys, after the use of jockeys under 16 was banned in 2004. Camel racing is a lucrative but dangerous sport, and has been linked to the kidnap and selling of children as young as four years old.

A pregnant camel is known as a git.

The word 'git' comes from the Arabic for pregnant camel, and was picked up by British servicemen in Egypt during the Second World War. However it's likely they only noticed the word because 'git' or 'get' – meaning a 'bastard' or 'fool' – was already part of Army slang.

Persian Greyhound dogs were trained to hunt on camels.

Known as the 'Royal Dog of Egypt', Salukis would lie on the camels' necks in front of their masters, watching for gazelle or oryx in the desert. They would then leap off in pursuit when they saw their prey, preserving their energy for the quick chase needed to catch the animal. The Saluki is an ancient breed and much prized by the Bedouins, who allow it to sleep in their tents. This is because the Islamic rules regarding cleanliness do not apply to the Saluki, as they are not classed as dogs, but are believed to be gifts from God.

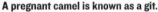

Camels originate from North America.

Fossil evidence indicates the ancestors of modern camels evolved in North America during the Palaeogene period, with the ancestors of the desert animal even living in Alaska. The earliest known camel-like animals were the size of rabbits and lived 40 million years ago, with later camels developing longer necks and limbs for crossing the expanding grassland of the time. As the animals evolved they spread to South America and later to most parts of Asia.

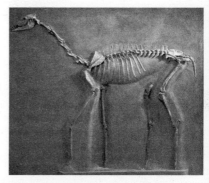

A camel and llama crossbreed is called a 'cama'.

The first cama, called Rama, was bred by British scientist Dr Julian Skidmore in Dubai in 1998. The aim was to combine the best features of both animals, such as the strength of the camel and the long coat and cooperative temperament of the llama, although Rama was reported to have a filthy temper.

CARROTS

The orange carrot only came about because patriotic Dutch growers bred the vegetable to grow in the colours of the House of Orange.

The first carrots were white, purple, red, yellow, green and black – not orange. The modern orange carrot was developed by Dutch growers in the 16–17th centuries, evidenced from variety names and contemporary artworks.

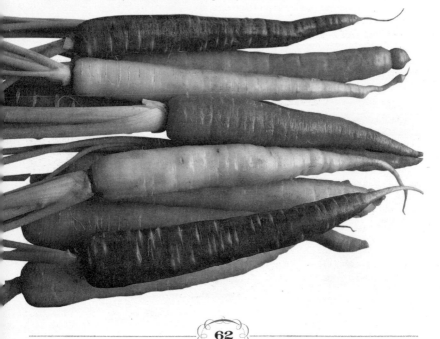

Carrots are effective against dandruff.

Carrots also help in stimulating milk flow during lactation.

In Scotland, the Sunday before Michaelmas – 29 September – is called 'Carrot Sunday'.

The carrot was a fertility symbol usually given by a woman to her intended husband. On the afternoon of the Sunday preceding Michaelmas, women and girls in the Hebrides gather St Michael's wild carrots. As the carrots are being dug, the following charm is recited:

Cleft, fruitful, fruitful, fruitful,
Joy of carrots surpassing upon me
Michael the brave endowing me
Bride the fair be aiding me.

Carrots contain more sugar than any other vegetable, with the exception of sugar beets.

When the British Navy blockaded West Indian sugar from entering Europe in the 18th century, chemists made sugar from organic carrots. The resulting thick syrup refuses to crystallise, and in competition with either cane sugar or that obtained from the sugar beet, it has not proved commercially successful.

The longest carrot recorded was over 19 feet long.

According to the *Guinness Book of Records*, the world's longest carrot was 19 feet and 1.96 inches. It was grown in the UK by Joe Atherton in 2007. Also according to the *Guinness Book of Records* John Evans created the heaviest carrot, a whopping 18.985 pounds in 1998, a world record for a single root mass.

CATS

In 19th century Belgium, cats were employed to deliver letters.

In 1879 the Belgian city of Liege employed 37 cats to carry bundles of letters to villages in return for saucers of milk. The *New York Times* reported: 'Messages are to be fastened in water-proof bags around the necks of the animals, and it is believed that, unless the criminal class of dogs undertakes to waylay and rob the mail cats, the messages will be delivered rapidly and safely.' Sadly the experiment was short-lived as the cats proved 'undisciplined'. Author Gretchen Lamont has written a book inspired by the incident entitled *The Mail-Carrier Cats of Liège*.

According to his rival Wagner, the composer Brahms hated cats so much that he would sit at his window in Vienna and shoot at them with a home-made harpoon manufactured from a bow and arrow.

Wagner started this rumour as a taunt to the quality of Brahms' music, stating that Brahms wanted to reproduce the cats' death cries to enhance his compositions.

In the 17th century, people would stuff wicker effigies of the Pope with live cats and then burn them.

The earliest recorded Pope burning demonstration took place in London in 1673, in protest at the unpopular marriage of James Duke of York and the Catholic Mary of Modena. In 1677, a lively Pope burning is recorded as having included two devils accompanying the Pope, whispering in his ear, wine distributed to the crowd to encourage a festive atmosphere, and cats in the Pope's belly, whose dying shrieks were said to mimic the Pope's dialogue with the devils.

Knowing the Egyptians worshipped cats, the Persians threw dozens of them over the walls of an Egyptian fort they were besieging.

They also threw other sacred animals, such as dogs, sheep and ibis birds, and rather than risk harm to their gods, the Egyptians surrendered. This was during the key Battle of Pelusium in 525 BC, after which the Persians conquered Egypt.

In Liverpool in March 1890, 18,000 mummified cats were sold as fertiliser.

Nine tonnes of the cats, from a catacomb at the cemetery of Beni Hasan, were auctioned off. Bidding started at £3 per tonne and the auctioneer used one of the cat's heads as a hammer.

HORRIBLE RESULT OF USING THE "EGYPTIAN FUR-TILISER."

CHAMPAGNE

Table tennis was originally played with balls made from champagne corks.

The game was a popular after-dinner amusement among the upper classes in the late 1800s. British officers reportedly first used champagne cork balls and cigar box bats over a net of books in 1881.

The longest recorded champagne cork flight was 177 feet and 9 inches.

American Heinrich Medicus ejected the cork from level ground at Woodbury Vineyards in New York in 1988. He said that he achieved this record-breaking distance by combining his skills as a physicist, meteorologist and former artillerist. The record for the most champagne corks popped simultaneously is 2,778.

Printer ink is more expensive than vintage champagne.

A typical Hewlett-Packard inkjet printer cartridge costs £17 for 5 ml or £3,400 per litre, compared with Dom Pérignon 2003 vintage champagne, which costs £146.65 per litre".

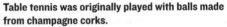

HP Colour Ink: £3,400.00 per litre
(HP300 Colour Ink 5ml: £17.00)

Epson Colour Ink: £3,074.29 per litre
(Epson T098 Colour Ink 3.5ml: £10.76)

Bollinger: £56.65 per litre
(Bollinger Special Cuvee Brut 75cl: £42.49)

Dom Perignon Vintage: £146.65 per litre
(Dom Perignon Blanc 2003 Vintage 75cl: £109.99)

Chanel No. 5 Spray Perfume: £,1340.00 per litre
(50ml: £67.00)

Moisturiser: Clarins: £800.00 per litre
(Clarins Multi-Active Day Cream 50ml: £40.00)

Grey Goose Vodka: £51.43 per litre
(Grey Goose Vodka 70cl: £36.00)

Max Factor Nail Polish: £886.67 per litre
(Max Factor Colour Effects 4.5ml: £3.99)

A play at the Globe Theatre in London in 1870 had to be called off before the interval, after the cast became too inebriated to continue during a picnic scene in Act One which included real champagne.

The audience at the two-year-old Globe Theatre in London witnessed 'disgraceful scenes' at a performance of Lord Newry's play *Ecarte*. During the lengthy picnic scene the cast 'partook of a substantial repast washed down with copious champagne which soon reduced them to a state of mild intoxication' causing them to forget their lines, knock over scenery and even fall asleep. Responding to the derision of the audience, the play's leading lady stumbled to the footlights and announced: 'Now, you stupid fools, when you have done laughing and making idiots of yourselves, I will go on with this beastly play'. The audience wouldn't let her.

A raisin dropped in a glass of fresh champagne will bob up and down continually from the bottom of the glass to the top.

This movement is due to the dissolved carbon dioxide in the liquid; the CO_2 bubbles attach to the surface of the raisin, and lift the raisin to the top. When the bubbles escape into the air, the raisins sink again, and the process continues until all the CO_2 has been used up.

CHEESE

Chihuahua cheese is popular in Mexico.

Queso Chihuahua is a soft white cow's milk cheese, named after the Mexican state from which it originates. It's similar to a mild white cheddar, and is available in braids, balls or rounds.

A Parisian grocer was jailed for stabbing his wife with a wedge of hard cheese.

Othello Federici was jailed for two years after he used a wedge of frozen Parmesan cheese to stab his wife in 1976.

An Irish chieftain nicknamed Cheese-Guzzler O'Ruairc died of 'a surfeit of sex'.

Mant na Mulchán Ua Ruairc, King of the Glaisfhéine, was captured by his enemies in 1204 and blinded as punishment. The archives tell how 'a woman was brought to him whilst he lay suffering from the operation, and shared his company; and he died soon after'. The clan of O'Ruaircs are the forbears of today's O'Rourkes, and *mulchán* is the Middle Irish for cheese.

In Vermont, apple pie must legally be served with a cheese topping.

In 1999, Vermont passed a law designating the apple as the state fruit and apple pie as state pie. The law also requires restaurants to serve apple pie with either a glass of milk, a scoop of vanilla ice cream or a slice of cheddar cheese weighing a minimum of half an ounce. Between June 1935 and March 1937, it was a legal requirement in Wisconsin to serve cheese and butter with every meal in a restaurant, no matter what was ordered.

The structure of the Moon is closer to that of cheese than to earth rocks.

A paper in the journal *Science* in 1970 showed that seismological studies have revealed that moon 'rock' is considerably less dense than any type of rock found on earth. The scientists also examined various cheeses, and found that the seismic velocity of these cheeses, especially Italian Romano, Vermont cheddar and Wisconsin Muenster, were much closer to the lunar basalt samples than any rock found on earth.

CHICKENS

One of the closest living relatives of the Tyrannosaurus Rex is the chicken.

Protein extracted from 68-million-year-old T-Rex bones recovered in 2003 was analysed by researchers who compared organic molecules preserved in fossils with those of living animals, and found that T-Rex collagen makeup is almost identical to that of the modern chicken.

For 3,000 years in Britain chickens were farmed primarily for their eggs. Only when the Romans came to Britain did it dawn on them to eat the bird.

The Ancient British would have eaten the eggs rather than kill the chicken so that the food source would be maintained.

In 1902, Andrew Jackson Jr of Tennessee patented a pair of miniature glasses for chickens.

They served as an eye protector for chickens to stop them being hen-pecked.

One variety used rose-coloured lenses as the colouring was thought to prevent a chicken wearing them from recognizing blood on other chickens which may increase the tendency for abnormal injurious behaviour.

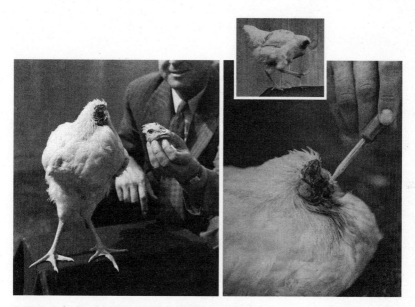

A chicken can live for up to two years without its head.

In 1945, a cockerel in Colorado had his head chopped off and lived. Incredibly, the axe had missed the jugular vein and left enough of the brainstem attached to the neck for him to survive, even thrive. Mike, as he was known, became a national celebrity, touring the country and featuring in *Time* and *Life* magazines. At the height of his fame, Mike was making $4,500 a month, and was valued at $10,000.

Chickens are among the bird world's most embarrassingly poor aviators. The longest recorded flight of a chicken is 13 seconds.

Sheena, a barnyard bantam, flew 630 feet, 2 inches for the longest known chicken flight.

CHILDBIRTH

The heaviest baby ever recorded at birth weighed over 22 pounds.

According to the *Guinness Book of Records*, Carmelina Fedele of Italy set the world record for the heaviest baby in 1955 when she gave birth to a 22-pound 8-ounce boy. The baby pictured is little Ademilton dos Santos of Brazil, who weighed in at a mere 17 pounds.

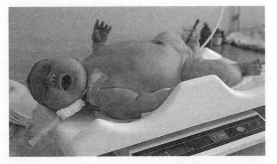

The record for most babies born to a single woman is 69.

The mother of this remarkable brood was the first wife of 18th century Russian peasant Feodor Vassilyev, who had 27 pregnancies, resulting in 16 pairs of twins, seven sets of triplets and four sets of quadruplets. Vassilyev went on to have a further 18 children by his second wife, making him the father of 87. These births were recorded by the Monastery of Nikolsk, and the records also show that only three of his children died in infancy.

There have been several recorded cases of babies that have been delivered through the rectum.

Spontaneous deliveries can bypass the vagina. This is technically known as a third- or fourth-degree episiotomy.

Most babies cry in the key of 'A'.

In 1994, Dr Philip Zeskind, a developmental psychologist at Virginia Polytechnic Institute, used a sophisticated acoustical analysis to determine that the ordinary cry of a baby is near the note 'A' below middle 'C'. He also noted that as the pitch of a baby's cry increases, parents experience a heightened sense of urgency to respond.

The world's youngest recorded mother gave birth at the age of five.

Lina Medina of Peru holds the record as the world's youngest mother, giving birth to a son Gerardo on 14 May 1939 when only five years old. Lina married in 1972 and gave birth to her second child that same year – 33 years after Gerardo had been born.

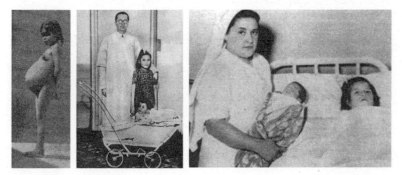

CHINA

China, Europe's second largest country after Belgium, is notable for having the longest-running production of *Hello Dolly* outside the West End.

In ancient times the Chinese would use the lining of a cat's stomach as a condom, hence their enormous population. This method was later refined when someone had the bright idea of removing the stomach from the cat first. But by then it was too late.

The Chinese are famous for their love of cheese. In fact the word comes from the Chinese word 'Chi' meaning a lump of solidified rancid milk. In Europe, this luxury item became known by the plural of 'Chi', which is of course 'Cheddar'.

When the Irish adventurer Marc O'Polo arrived in 15th century China he was delighted to discover exotic items like mints with holes in them, garlic, football pools, spaghetti and even macaroni; in fact it's widely believed that Marco Polo took the recipe for pasta back to Italy where it immediately caught on. For the Chinese, rice is their staple, although they are always looking for better ways to hold their sheets of paper together.

Among the many things we take for granted in our day to day life, it may be surprising to learn that it was the Chinese who invented pop-tarts, the lottery rollover, focus groups and perforations.

Had perforations been readily available in 1393 when toilet paper was first introduced for the use of the Emperor, the individual sheets might not have measured 2 feet by 3 feet.

Another Chinese invention is the colour 'beige'. It was previously known as 'peek'. The capital city takes its name from the beige dye makers of the area who specialise in dull pale brownish colours, popular with the cardigan makers of Shanghai.

Of course trade with the West is completely one way, as China accepts no foreign imports at all due to obvious reasons combined with unforeseen problems. For example, in China the slogan 'Come alive with Pepsi' was misinterpreted as: 'Pepsi Brings Your Relatives Back From The Dead'.

China is the only country where you can get jet-lag on foot. If you stepped across the border from China to Afghanistan you would lose 3½ hours.

The Chinese people take great pride in the fact that the Great Wall of China is the only man-made structure on Earth from which you can see the Moon.

FACT ⊙ : In ancient times the Chinese would use the lining of a cat's stomach as a condom.

FACT ⊙ : It's widely believed that Marco Polo took the recipe for pasta back to Italy where it immediately caught on.

FACT ⊙ : Had perforations been readily available in 1393 when toilet paper was first introduced for the use of the Emperor, the individual sheets might not have measured 2 feet by 3 feet.

FACT ⊙ : In China the slogan 'Come alive with Pepsi' was misinterpreted as: 'Pepsi Brings Your Relatives Back From The Dead'.

FACT ⊙ : China is the only country where you can get jet-lag on foot. If you stepped across the border from China to Afghanistan you would lose 3½ hours.

CHOCOLATE

Chaka Khan has her own range of chocolates called 'Chakalates'.

The Chakalates are available from her website, and proceeds from sales go to the Chaka Khan Foundation.

A German man took legal action against the Easter Bunny, accusing him of promoting addiction to chocolate causing grievous bodily harm.

Karl-Friedrich Lentze, from Berlin, filed the complaint in 2006, accusing the Bunny of causing chocolate addiction, leading to heart attacks, obesity and strokes. Lentze called the Easter Bunny an 'unscrupulous and sadistic offender', and called on prosecutors to find the creature and 'handcuff his paws'. Public prosecutor spokesman Christian Avenarius assured the public that they would act on the complaint 'with speed and diligence'.

The microwave oven was invented after a radar tube melted a chocolate bar in a researcher's pocket.

Shortly after the end of the Second World War, the American engineer and inventor Percy Spencer was touring one of his laboratories at the Raytheon Company in Massachusetts. He stopped momentarily in front of a magnetron, the power tube that drives a radar set. Feeling a sudden and strange sensation, Spencer noticed that the chocolate bar in his pocket had begun to melt. After finding that popcorn popped in front of the machine too, he went on to patent the microwave oven.

A cockatoo from Nuneaton spent two weeks trying to hatch a bowl of Cadbury's Creme Eggs.

The 17-year-old bird called Pippa adopted the chocolate eggs when her owner put them out before Easter as a treat for visitors to a Warwickshire wildlife centre. The bird's owner, Geoff Grewcock, said Pippa saw the eggs on a table and immediately began nesting on them. When they failed to hatch, she started pecking at them, apparently to speed the process. The bird became so possessive of the eggs that Mr Grewcock could only remove them one by one.

You can buy a bra crafted entirely out of chocolate.

Austrian designer Reinlinde Trummer has produced the world's first bra made entirely of chocolate. It sells for approximately £100 and Trummer claims it doesn't melt on the wearer.

CIRCUSES

The first human cannon ball was a 14-year-old girl called Zazel.

In 1877, Zazel used a cannon that was mechanised with elastic bands connected to a platform inside the cannon to propel herself into the sky. Her 60-foot flight caused such a sensation she made a living out of it. Human cannon balls today prefer to use a system that applies compressed air as the means of propulsion. Since Zazel's time, more than 30 UK stuntmen have been killed in the process, mostly by missing the net. The most famous cannon balling act were the Zacchini brothers who began in 1922, but suffered catastrophe when one brother broke his back after a mid-air collision with another brother, having been shot from opposite ends of the circus ring.

The Department of Clown Registry protects a clown's make-up from being copied by painting each clown's distinctive face onto a goose egg.

The fee is currently $18.95. Linda McBryde is the manager of the Department of Clown Registry in Buchanan, Virginia. Linda carefully uses acrylic paint to recreate the clown's face on a goose egg from a close-up photograph.

Johnny Depp, P. Diddy, Daniel Radcliffe and Billy Bob Thornton are all scared of clowns.

They all suffer from 'coulrophobia', a fear of clowns and circus performers. In an interview with the *Courier Mail*, Depp said his fear stems from their painted smiles, which make it impossible 'to distinguish if they are happy or if they're about to bite your face off', and P. Diddy has a strict 'No Clown' clause in his performance agreements.

In 1972, the owner of a circus elephant called Bimbo was awarded $4,500 in damages by a California court after a traffic accident caused the animal to lose interest in dancing and water-skiing.

Ten years before, *Life* magazine reported Bimbo's talents for water-skiing on quarter-tonne skis. Bimbo wasn't the only elephant who has been trained to water-ski; Queenie found fame at a Florida theme park in the 50s and 60s, where she also played the harmonica.

Technically, the act of knife throwing is known as the 'impalement arts', despite the whole aim to be avoiding impalement.

However, the use of arrows in the impalement arts contravenes the rules of archery in the UK.

CLEOPATRA

Egyptian coins of the time depict Cleopatra as a woman with a hooked nose and a masculine face.

Archaeologists recently discovered a 2,000-year-old coin bearing the images of Cleopatra and Mark Antony. Cleopatra had a shallow forehead, pointed chin, thin lips, a witch-like nose and appears not to have put her teeth in. Mark Antony fares little better; he had peculiar bulging eyes, a hook nose and an incredibly thick neck. Roman historians tell us that Cleopatra was intelligent and charismatic with a seductive voice but, curiously, make no mention of her beauty at all.

Cleopatra was the offspring of a brother and sister, and married two of her brothers.

Cleopatra's father, Ptolemy XII, and her mother, Cleopatra V, were half brother and sister. The right to rule went through the female line, so Egyptian politics dictated that royal brothers married royal sisters to cement their position. Also, as divine beings, only other royals were good enough to marry and procreate, so incest was common and considered quite acceptable. Cleopatra took a consort at the age of 11, when she married her younger brother, Ptolemy XIII. Ptolemy later died fighting against Julius Caesar's army, when he is thought to have drowned in the Nile.

Cleopatra decreed that earthworms were sacred, and removing one from Egypt was an offence punishable by death.

The pioneering 18th century English naturalist Gilbert White wrote of the earthworm's ability to fertilise the soil: 'the earth without worms would soon become cold, hard-bound, and void of fermentation, and consequently sterile'. It appears Cleopatra had already made this discovery, as Egyptians were forbidden to remove any worm from the land, and farmers were not to disturb worms for fear of stunting the renowned fertility of the Nile Valley's soil.

WHAT LONDON LOOKS LIKE WHEN THE AIR-HUNS COME ON THEIR MISSIONS OF MURDER.

In 1917, during the First World War, Cleopatra's Needle became the first monument in London to be hit during an air raid.

Cleopatra's Needle was presented to the British in 1819 by the Turkish Viceroy of Egypt, and six men died during its voyage to Britain, when it was nearly lost during a storm in the Bay of Biscay. At its base lies a time capsule containing a selection of British currency, a railway guide and photographs of the 12 best-looking women in England.

'Cleopatra' was Ronnie Wood's nickname at school.

This was due to his prominent nose, a feature he shared with the ancient ruler.

COCA-COLA

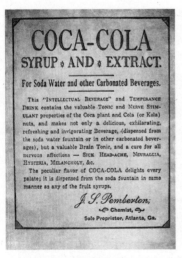

Coca-Cola was first sold as a medicine capable of curing morphine addiction, dyspepsia, neurasthenia, headache and impotence.

The price of the first serving of Coca-Cola in 1886 was five cents (about a dollar in today's money) and this price didn't change for 70 years. Coke's inventor, John Pemberton, himself addicted to morphine, claimed his product could cure many diseases.

Coca-Cola once contained an estimated nine milligrams of cocaine per glass.

Pemberton used five ounces of coca leaf per gallon of syrup, which was a significant dose. Three glasses a day, plus the accelerator effect of the caffeine, was more than the average 20 to 30 milligrams snorted by a contemporary cocaine user. In 1903 the cocaine was removed.

The name Coca-Cola in China was first rendered as 'Ke-kou-ke-la'. Unfortunately, the phrase means 'bite the wax tadpole' or 'female horse stuffed with wax', depending on the dialect.

It was all the fault of Chinese shopkeepers who, anticipating Coke's entry to the market, produced advertising material that rendered the name Coca-Cola into Mandarin characters with no regard to the meaning of the phrase the sounds produced. Coke later found a close phonetic equivalent, 'ko-kou-ko-le', which can be loosely translated as: 'to allow the mouth to be able to rejoice'.

In 1379, a Mr and Mrs Coke of Yorkshire named their daughter 'Diot'.

The discovery was made by a researcher at the National Archives. 'Diot' was a Christian name for girls in the 14th century, short for Dionisia.

A can of Diet Coke will float in water while a can of regular Coke sinks.

A can of regular Coke sinks because it is denser than water, while less-dense Diet Coke floats.

COCKROACHES

Even though cockroaches have been on the earth for 350 million years, they have not changed at all.

The earliest cockroach-like fossils date from the Carboniferous Period, some 350 million years ago, and fossil records indicate that they were the predominant insects during this period.

Cockroaches break wind every 15 minutes.

Insect flatulence may account for one-fifth of all the methane emissions on the planet. One academic paper has described this 15-minute farting cycle as a 'peak emission', suggesting that the cockroach may in fact be popping them out on an even more regular basis.

In Brazil, there's a species of cockroach that eats eyelashes. It has a preference for those of young children, and usually feeds while they are asleep.

The insect is attracted to minerals and moisture from the eye's tear ducts, but it has been known to go for other areas of the body that produce moisture also.

A cockroach can live for a month without its head.

The insect only dies because it can't drink any water without a mouth; cockroaches can survive for two to three months on water alone. Cockroaches do not have blood pressure like mammals do, so the neck wound clots before the insect bleeds to death, and cockroaches also breathe through spiracles in their body segments, rather than through the mouth.

There is a cockroach museum, called the 'Cockroach Hall Of Fame', in Plano, Texas. It features record-breaking cockroaches, and insects dressed as famous people.

The museum was founded by pest control specialist Michael Bohdan, and is housed in his 'Pest Shop'. Exhibits include cockroaches dressed like stars such as Elvis, Marilyn Monroe and Liberace.

COMPETITIONS

In 1994, a woman won a car by kissing it for 32 hours and 20 minutes.

23-year-old waitress Alice Johnson from Santa Fe loosened four teeth in the process of kissing the car bonnet.

PASSION WAGON

CONTESTANTS paid more than lip service in a Santa Fe competition to win a car – by kissing it. Waitress Alice Johnson, 23, was "tyred" but happy after puckering up for 32 hours and 20 minutes – although four teeth had worked loose en route.

Jose Luis Astoreka won the world's first competition for 'cracking walnuts in the anus' after he succeeded in cracking an impressive 30 walnuts in 57 seconds.

The competition took place in the Spanish village of Kortezubi in 1990. His brother, Juan Ramon, was second with a time of 1 minute 20 seconds. The brothers' winning times have been attributed to 'a peculiar physical characteristic which runs in the Astoreka family'.

Writer Graham Greene once came second in a 1949 'write like Graham Greene' contest.

His entry was entitled 'The Stranger's Hand', and was submitted under the pen name 'N. Wilkinson'. Similarly, during the 1920s, Charlie Chaplin once went to a Charlie Chaplin-look-alike competition in San Francisco, but didn't even make it to the finals. Other stars who have successfully disguised themselves include Paul McCartney, who in 1984 donned dark glasses and went busking in London's Leicester Square Tube station. He only made a few pounds, but donated this to charity. Sting has also worn a disguise to go busking. He made £40 for his efforts, and one woman recognised him, although she was silenced by a man behind her in the crowd who told her, 'You silly cow, it's not him, he's a multi-millionaire.'

In 1997, Mary Esposito won the US title of 'most infested home' after her apartment was infested by 75,000 cockroaches.

Her prize was $1,000 and a supply of cockroach-control products. Ms Esposito said that the creatures lived all over the house, including in her dishwasher, fridge, oven, coffee maker, VCR, wallpaper and taps, but maintained that she kept a clean home.

This just in . . .

Woman wins $1,000 prize for roach-infested home

FOREST PARK, Ga. (AP) — For 18 months, Mary Esposito had to share her home with an estimated 60,000 uninvited guests.

That's how many roaches that entomologist Austin Frishman believes infested Esposito's home in this Atlanta suburb. He spent Tuesday getting rid of them as part of a demonstration freebie.

Esposito said breaks in the floor let roaches enter her kitchen, making their home in her dishwasher, dresser drawers, even her VCR.

"I've tried everything, and nothing has worked," she said.

In April, she saw a newspaper advertisement by Combat Insect Control Systems saying, "Your roaches could make you rich."

"I certainly have enough of them, so I thought, 'Why not?'" she said.

She got lucky. Her home was selected as one of six winners from more than 1,000 entries from 41 states. She won $1,000 and a free treatment by Frishman.

In the sport of finch-sitting, competitors put a male finch in a cage for an hour, and whoever's finch chirps the most in an hour is the winner.

Known as *vinkenzetting* in its native Flanders, the sport can trace its origins to competitions held by Flemish merchants in 1596, and is considered an important part of Flemish culture. Meeting in car parks or on streets, competitors place their cages in a row six feet apart, as the close proximity increases the number of calls. A winning bird can be expected to make several hundred calls per hour, although one bird owner was accused of doping with testosterone after his entry called 1,278 times. Another scandal was discovered after a bird sang the exact same number of calls in two rounds, and a mini CD player was found in the cage.

COMPUTERS

The Vatican has three host computers called Raphael, Michael and Gabriel.

Named after the archangels, these computers are the Vatican's net servers, powering their eight-language website and dedicated YouTube channel. In 2004 it was claimed that the Vatican website suffered 10,000 virus attacks and 900 attempted hackings every month.

The world's first office computer was used by Lyons Tea Houses.

In 1951 the management of Joseph Lyons tea houses built their own computer named LEO, short for Lyons Electronic Office. The computer occupied 5,000 square feet at the firm's Cadby Hall headquarters in Hammersmith, and its first task - the world's first business computing application - was to calculate the costs of Lyons' weekly bakery distribution run.

GUINNESS WORLD RECORDS

CERTIFICATE

The first ever business computer was LEO I (Lyons Electronic Office).

It began operations in November 1951 at the Lyons headquarters, London, UK.

A computer error resulted in 41,000 Parisians who'd committed parking offences being sent letters charging them with murder, extortion and organised prostitution.

Recipients were reportedly 'surprised' by the contents of the letters sent out on 6 September 1989, some of which also contained charges of drug trafficking and deviant sexual practices. The misprints were allegedly caused by an 'error' in the court computer system.

The 'mouse mouse' is a computer mouse housed inside the dead carcass of a real mouse.

Americans Christy Canida and Noah Weinstein created the 'mouse mouse' from the skin of a dead rodent bought from a pet shop, and have published a how-to guide on the internet to enable others to make their own. The guide recommends users obtain a pale furred animal which is already dead, and contains useful tips, such as: 'it's easier to fit a small object into a large mouse than a large object into a small mouse'.

In computing terminology, half a byte is called a nybble.

Sometimes spelt 'nibble', it is used to designate the left-most, or right-most, four bits of a byte.

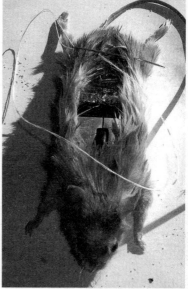

COWS

In Sweden there's a train that runs on methane, which is collected from the stewed organs of cows.

A tanker takes the stinking cow organs from the abbatoir to a bio-gas factory, where they are stewed gently for a month before the methane can be drawn off. The stewed organs of one cow will get the train about 4 km along the tracks.

Cows are often fed magnets to reduce the damage caused by the metal objects they regularly swallow.

'Hardware disease' is the name for the inflammation caused by the wire, staples and nails they swallow, which can result in lower milk production in dairy cows. The farmer feeds a magnet to each calf at branding time. The magnet settles in the rumen or reticulum of the animal and remains there for the life of the animal.

Despite eating only grass, cows have two and a half times as many taste buds as humans.

Humans have about 8-10,000 taste buds on their tongue while cows have around 25,000. Pigs and similar omnivores have 15,000, cats 470 and chickens a mere 50.

Cows each burp 600 pints of methane a day and are responsible for a third of the UK's greenhouse gas emissions.

Cow burps are responsible for 4 per cent of worldwide greenhouse gas emissions and a third of the UK's. Livestock farming in general creates 18 per cent of all man-made greenhouse gases – more than all the cars and other forms of transport on earth. Cows produce one pound of methane for every two pounds of meat they yield. 600 pints of methane each day is enough to heat a small house. Argentine scientists have been strapping plastic tanks to the backs of cows to collect their burps.

Cows moo in regional accents.

Language specialists say cows have regional accents like humans. They decided to examine the issue after dairy farmers noticed their cows had slightly different moos, depending on which herd they came from. John Wells, Professor of Phonetics at the University of London, said regional twangs had been seen before in birds. Farmer Lloyd Green, from Glastonbury, said: 'I spend a lot of time with my cows and they definitely moo with a Somerset drawl.'

CRICKET

The Admiralty Islanders in the Pacific make their cricket bats from the wood of a tree grown from the artificial leg of the missionary Elisha Fawcett, who first brought them the game.

The early 19th-century one-legged Manchester missionary Elisha Fawcett devoted his life to teaching the Commandments of God and the Laws of Cricket to the natives of the Pacific Island. When Fawcett died, his wooden leg was used as a tombstone. It took root and its wood was used to make cricket bats for generations thereafter.

In 1796, a team of one-legged cricketers defeated a one-armed team by 103 runs.

The retired sailors from Greenwich played the match for a 1,000-guinea prize, and the one-legged men even had enough energy left afterwards to compete in a hundred-yard running race. The match was repeated in 1841, and on a number of occasions after that, establishing a tradition.

THE ONE ARM AND ONE LEG CRICKET MATCH AT LORDS.

Australian Rules football was originally designed to give cricketers something to play during the off-season.

English public school-educated Thomas Wentworth Wills devised the sport as a way of keeping cricket players fit through the winter, and the first recorded game was played in 1858.

Ladies used blue cricket balls during Edwardian times.

It is thought the use of blue cricket balls was to avoid the inevitable over excitement the ladies would experience at the sight of red balls. In the late 1980s, the men's game experimented with an orange ball, but this was discontinued as TV companies found it did not show up properly on screen.

Snow stopped play in a county cricket match between Derbyshire and Lancashire in June 1975.

According to the Met Office, the inch of snow that fell on the pitch was caused by a depression moving down from the Arctic, but the thaw that followed brought a gloriously hot summer.

CROCODILES

Crocodilopolis was a city in Ancient Egypt.
It was named by the Greeks due to the particular reverence paid by its inhabitants to crocodiles, in particular 'Sobek' the crocodile god. The city worshipped a sacred crocodile called 'Petsuchos', or 'Son of Sobek', that was embellished with gold and gems, and lived in a special temple.

In Ancient Egypt, crocodile dung was used as a contraceptive.
Documents dating back to 1850 BC refer to women using crocodile dung pessaries, which may have worked as, like modern-day spermicides, crocodile dung is slightly alkaline. However, the Ancient Egyptians also believed that a mixture of acacia dates and honey could prevent a woman getting pregnant for up to three years.

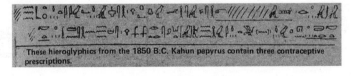

These hieroglyphics from the 1850 B.C. Kahun papyrus contain three contraceptive prescriptions.

Adult crocodiles can go up to two years without eating.

San Diego Zoo says that some large adults can possibly make it longer, as they store fat in their tails. Some crocodile species can also eat up to half their body weight in one meal, hold their breath underwater for over an hour, and swim at 20 mph.

For crocodiles up to two metres long, an ordinary rubber band should be sufficient to hold their jaws shut.

It's because their muscles are set to maximise the ability to clamp the jaw shut, which means the muscles giving the croc the ability to open its jaw are contrastingly weak.

Prince Waldemar of Prussia once released a crocodile into Queen Victoria's study at Buckingham Palace.

He was the Queen's grandson, and is reported to have enjoyed collecting fossils on the Isle of Wight, and terrifying his grandmother with his pet crocodile. Sadly, the Prince died aged 11.

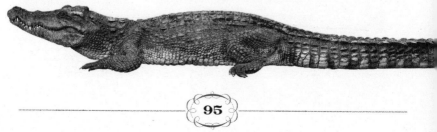

CURRY

In 1912, Wilbur Scoville invented a scientific scale with which to measure the heat of chillies.

The Scoville scale is a measure of the 'hotness' of a chilli pepper and is still used today. Scoville's process was actually quite simple; a chilli was added to a sugar and water solution, which was then diluted until the solution no longer tasted 'hot'. The level of dilution needed was made into the scale we use today. However, many have questioned its precision, as it relies on subjective taste.

In 2003, Sharwoods launched a 'Bundh' range of sauces, not realising that the literal translation of the Punjabi *bund* is 'arse' or 'anus'.

Sharwoods spent £6 million to advertise the launch of the sauces, which they promised were 'deliciously rich'. Sharwoods said they were 'dismayed' by the mistake, but pointed out the name was pronounced differently.

HOW HOT IS THAT CHILLI?

Naga Viper pepper — 1,500,000
1,000,000
800,000
Red Savina Habanero
500,000
350,000
200,000
Habanero Chili
Orange Habanero
Scotch Bonnet
100,000
70,000 — Bird's Eye Chili
Cayenne — 50,000
Tabasco
30,000
6,000
3,000 — Jalapeño
1,000 — Poblano
Pepperoncini —
500
200 — Banana
100
Bell

Sharwoods Bundh
IT TASTES LOUD

Britain exports chicken tikka masala to India.

Chicken tikka masala originated in the UK, and in 2009 MP Mohammad Sarwar tabled an early day motion in the House of Commons asking that parliament support a campaign for Glasgow to be given European Union protected designation of origin status for chicken tikka masala.

In Swiss versions of the board game 'Cluedo', Colonel Mustard is known as Madame Curry.

Madame Curry's card in the board game depicts her as a white-haired lady sipping tea.

In Japan you can buy a soft drink called 'Ramune' in a lemonade and curry flavour.

Ramune is known for its distinctive bottle, which is sealed with a marble, and its unusual flavours, which include wasabi, octopus, 'disco dance' and 'mystery'.

CUTLERY

In Elizabethan England, the spoon was such a rarity that people carried their own folding spoons to banquets.

Spoons were a sort of status symbol, and they were often ornate. The Romans had folding 'eating utensils' 1,500 years earlier.

In 17th century England, forks were considered an insult to God.

The Catholic Church disapproved of the use of forks, since God had provided man with fingers to eat with, such practices were seen as 'excessive delicacy', and forks were associated with sinful courtesans.

Until the late 19th century British sailors were forbidden to use forks as they were considered unmanly and harmful to discipline.

In England, the use of forks was for many years viewed as an 'unmanly Italian affectation', and as late as 1897 there are reports of some naval figures regarding forks as being 'prejudicial to discipline and manners'.

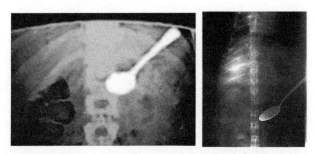

In 2006, in a restaurant in Sydney, Australia, a woman accidentally swallowed a 6-inch spoon.

The accident occurred while the woman was having a laughing fit as she ate a plate of spaghetti. Doctors at Sydney's Canterbury hospital eventually managed to remove the item by using snares to lasso the spoon and pull it out of her oesophagus and through her throat.

The first ice lolly dates back to a cold night in 1905, when Frank Epperson left a glass of lemonade with a spoon in it on a chilly windowsill.

Epperson was nine years old at the time, and enjoyed inventing and experimenting to make exotic drinks. He called his creation the Epperson Icicle, or Ep-sicle for short. He finally patented the invention in 1924, after his son had renamed it the Popsicle.

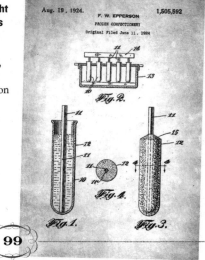

DANCING

In 1518, Strasbourg suffered a plague of dancing.

Around 400 citizens became afflicted in what is now regarded as an outbreak of mass hysteria, and as many as 50 people danced themselves to death. The origin is thought to lie in a Christian legend, which said that the martyred Saint Vitus would send plagues of compulsive dancing upon anyone who provoked his wrath. There have been outbreaks of dancing mania recorded throughout Europe from the 7th to the 17th centuries. An outbreak in 1278 ended in disaster after 200 people dancing on a bridge over the River Meuse in Germany caused it to collapse.

THE
DANCING
PLAGUE
THE STRANGE TRUE STORY OF AN
EXTRAORDINARY ILLNESS

JOHN WALLER

An old name for Irish dancing was 'door dancing'.

Performed on doors taken off their hinges or on round barrel tops, this form of dance was much more loose limbed than the stiff 'Riverdance' style synonymous with Irish dancing today.

The tango originated as a dance between two men.

There was such a shortage of women in expanding Buenos Aires at the time the tango emerged that the culture of same-sex dancing became exceptionally

strong. This was aided by the cultural shift created by European immigration, which meant that men and women dancing in close proximity came to be seen as scandalous. Same-sex dancing became so widespread that the Argentinean authorities banned men dancing together in public places in 1916.

Notorious highwayman Claude Duval was known to enjoy a dance with any ladies travelling in the coaches he held up.

Before taking to the road, Duval was the respectable French page of the Duke of Richmond, and it seems that some of those gentlemanly tendencies stayed with him. It is reported how, among similar incidents, he once stopped a coach in which a gentleman and his wife were travelling, and asked the lady to dance a coranto with him upon the nearby heath. He then asked the husband, who had watched the dance, to pay for his entertainment, and allowed the coach to proceed on after taking only £100 of the £400 the couple were carrying.

In 1973, ballet dancer Wayne Sleep completed an 'entrechat douze', the crossing and uncrossing of legs 12 times in mid air.

This broke the previous record of 10 leg crossings, held by famous Russian ballet dancer Veslav Nijinsky. Until Sleep was filmed completing the move in seven tenths of a second, many thought it impossible, as no dancer can stay off the ground for more than a second.

DIVORCE

In 1981, an Indonesian man was jailed for seven years for marrying 121 women.

In mitigation he pointed out that he had divorced 93 of them in the eyes of Muslim religious law, where '*thalak*' means to release (or abandon) a spouse.

A study of New York Marathon runners found that their divorce rate was three and a half times the national average.

Fred Lebow, the director of the New York Marathon, said that this was true for both male and female participants, and a poll taken in the Boston area found that 40 per cent of married runners who ran more than 70 miles a week got divorced. The theory is that marital satisfaction is negatively affected by high concentrations of independent leisure activities.

A man from southern Cambodia was more particular than most when it came to splitting his property equally with his wife: he sawed their house in half.

The man had been living in the house with his wife for 40 years prior to the divorce. The man removed his half of the house to his parents' property while his ex-wife continued to live in the precariously perched upright half.

In 1986, Gene and Lynda Ballard got divorced while skydiving at 120 mph over California.

The veteran skydivers were joined by their lawyer and six close friends for the occasion. 'Almost everything in our marriage was done around skydiving, so the divorce in the air seemed the natural thing to do,' Lynda explained.

A New York doctor asked for an extra $1.5 million in his divorce case as compensation for a kidney he had donated to his ex-wife.

Dr Richard Batista donated his kidney in 2001, hoping to both save his wife's life, and help turn around their strained marriage. However, medical ethicists agreed that his case didn't stand much of a chance, as in the US organs may not be bought, sold or ascribed monetary value. Donating an organ is a gift, meaning that the kidney legally belonged to his wife, and no doctors would perform the surgery that would enable her to give it back.

DOGS

Dogs have around 100 unique facial expressions.

These are mostly dependent on ear movement. Dog owners can learn to read these expressions over time if they get to know their dog's breed and physical features well.

In Massachusetts in 1692, two dogs were hung for witchcraft.

During the time of the Salem witch trials, the dogs were suspected as accomplices of witches after a girl said they had appeared to her as the devil's disciples and given her the evil eye.

In the 1870s, a Frenchman invented a tricycle powered by dogs on treadmills.

Monsieur Huret's contraption, called a cynosphere, consisted of treadmills fitted into two large rear wheels. However, development was soon halted following protests from The Society for the Protection of Animals.

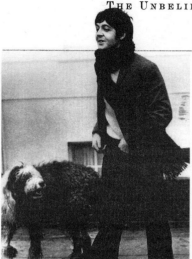

At the end of the Beatles' song 'A Day in the Life' there is an ultrasonic whistle, audible only to dogs.

The high-frequency 15 kilohertz tone features on the *Sgt. Pepper* album, alongside some studio chatter, and was recorded by Paul McCartney specially for his Shetland sheepdog.

The Dog Meat King restaurant in Beijing serves more than 50 different dog-based dishes.

Dog fondu, stir-fried dog chops and braised dog paws are specialities at the Sino-Korean 'Dog Meat King' restaurant, and St Bernards are regarded as a particular delicacy. However, the International Fund for Animal Welfare (IFAW) are outraged that St Bernards are being bred for their meat and have petitioned the Chinese government to introduce animal cruelty laws to stop the practice, saying it is as offensive as if the Swiss population took to eating Chinese pandas.

DONKEYS

'Donkey' is a surprisingly recent word. When the common use of the very old Anglo-Saxon word 'arse' was being supplemented by 'ass', especially in America, polite society started using 'donkey' so as to avoid being heard to accidentally swear.

In Ancient Egypt it was believed that the more donkeys you owned the higher your status. During the reign of Ptolemy, the entire Bank of Egypt's stock of donkeys stampeded, leading to galloping inflation. After that the currency became the more stable camel.

During the Middle Ages, the Christmas season sometimes saw the Feast of the Ass commemorating the donkey in the stable. On this day people were supposed to bray like a donkey at the points in the Mass where they would normally say 'Amen.'

A donkey has been crossed with a Shetland pony – the offspring is called a Shetland ponkey. A ponkey was then crossed with a Dwarf Miniature horse to produce an even smaller dinky donkey. A wee dinky donkey was then crossed with a ponkey to produce an attractive fridge magnet.

Harvey the Tap-Dancing Donkey toured the American Vaudeville circuit in the 1920s. He was noted for his Fred Astaire impressions and a lively buck and wing routine. He came to an unfortunate end at Pridey's Music Hall in Chicago. As luck would have it John Dillinger was snoozing in the audience when Harvey began his act, and on hearing the rat-a-tat of Harvey's hooves and mistaking it for a Thompson sub-machine gun, Dillinger returned fire and shot him dead.

Heston Blumenthal recently surprised restaurant guests with a donkey blancmange. The sweet, made with genuine donkey offal, was served in honour of Prince Andrew's birthday. Guests agreed that the confection tasted just like donkey offal.

In Brooklyn, New York, it is illegal for a donkey to sleep in a bathtub. It's possible to buy special bathtub alarms, to keep the donkey awake.

In Salem, Massachusetts, a donkey was strung up and put to death for taking part in witchcraft rituals. To this day any man suspected of immorality is liable to be hung like a donkey.

The chief witness in a 2007 court case in Dallas, Texas, was a donkey. Buddy was led into the courtroom to help resolve a dispute between two neighbours, but his evidence was dismissed as hearsay.

The Muffin Donkey Sanctuary on Hayling Island was closed by Health and Safety Officers from the RSPCA when they found that the donkeys were being allowed to smoke.

FACT ❶: When the common use of the very old Anglo-Saxon word 'arse' was being supplemented by 'ass', especially in America, polite society started using 'donkey', so as to avoid being heard to accidentally swear.

FACT ❷: In Ancient Egypt it was believed that the more donkeys you owned the higher your status.

FACT ❸: During the Middle Ages, the Christmas season saw the Feast of the Ass commemorating the donkey in the stable.

FACT ❹: In Brooklyn, New York, it is illegal for a donkey to sleep in a bathtub.

FACT ❺: The chief witness in a 2007 court case in Dallas, Texas, was a donkey.

DWARFS

The Romans regularly had dwarfs and women fighting against one another in the Coliseum.

Exotic wild animals from across the empire were also pitted against each other, as well as the usual gladiatorial combat and mass public executions. Sometimes the arena was even decorated with vast theatrical scenery to make it look like a desert or a forest. The Coliseum scene in Cecil B. DeMille's *The Sign of the Cross* includes the spectacle of Amazon women battling dwarfs.

The most famous dwarf spy was Richebourg, who was able to carry secret dispatches while disguised as an infant in his nurse's arms.

Less than two feet tall, he was employed by the aristocracy as a secret agent during the French Revolution, carrying secret military dispatches in and out of Paris concealed under his cap.

Charles I's favourite joke was to place his court dwarf between two halves of a loaf and pretend to eat him.

At 18 inches tall, Jeffrey Hudson was given as a present to Charles I's wife Henrietta Maria after he delighted her by jumping out of a pie dressed in a suit of armour at a banquet hosted by the Duke of Buckingham.

When circus dwarfs Lavinia Warren and Tom Thumb married, President Abraham Lincoln held a wedding reception for them that was attended by the entire United States Cabinet.

More than 2,000 guests attended their 'fairy wedding' in 1863, and it was considered the social event of the New York season. Barnum Circus received 15,000 requests for tickets to the wedding reception, where the couple greeted guests atop a grand piano.

SIR JEFFERY HUDSON
1619-1682
A DWARF PRESENTED IN A PIE
TO KING CHARLES 1ST.

Australian Adam Rainer is unique as having been classed as both a dwarf and a giant.

In 1920, at the age of 21, Rainer was officially a dwarf at just 3 feet 10 inches tall. However, he then experienced a massive growth spurt that left him weak and bedridden, and when he died at the age of 51 he was 7 feet 8 inches tall.

EARS

Of the 7.5 million people that use television subtitles in Britain, 6 million have no hearing impairment.

This research was carried out by the TV regulator OFCOM. It is thought that many hearing people use subtitles to help them keep up with complicated plot twists and unfamiliar accents in American TV dramas.

It's possible for humans to blow up balloons with their ears.

A 55-year-old factory worker from China noticed air leaking from his ears, and soon discovered he could inflate balloons and also blow out candles with the air he expelled from his ears. He is not the only one; 38-year-old Zhang Xijiang can do everything from smoking a cigarette to inflating bicycle tyres using nothing but his ears.

A human's hearing is less sharp after eating too much.

Recent studies published in the *New Scientist* magazine have shown that lifestyle has a noticeable impact on hearing loss. The inner ear is very sensitive to circulation problems, which can be caused by smoking and excess weight, both activities which decrease blood circulation. This is because hair cells in the inner ear die when they do not get enough oxygen and when toxic free radicals do not get transported away fast enough.

In 2010, a partially deaf man from Sheffield was cured after doctors removed a tooth that had been stuck in his ear canal for 33 years.

Ex-miner Stephen Hirst had suffered almost constant ear ache, partial deafness and frequent ear infections since he was 14, but it was only with the help of a suction tube and a pair of tweezers that doctors found the cause of the problem. Mr Hirst says he doesn't know how the tooth got in his ear, but guesses it might have been when he fell off a desk at school.

In the US, Noddy's friend Big Ears is called White Beard to avoid offending big-eared people.

In the American animated series of Enid Blyton's Noddy character, Noddy speaks with an American accent and Mr Plod the policeman becomes Officer Plod. Pleasing every sensitivity has proved difficult. When Toytown's black-skinned golliwogs became goblins in 1989 after complaints of racist overtones, protests were received from Scandinavian countries who believed their trolls were being insulted.

ELEPHANTS

Elephants are the only animals that humans have successfully trained to do headstands.

Although other primates can do headstands, elephants are the only animals humans have successfully trained to perform the feat. However, as this is not natural behaviour, many campaigners claim the practice is cruel to the elephants, and want to see it banned in entertainment venues.

The 'largest animal orchestra' is the Thai Elephant Orchestra of Lampang.

The orchestra is made up of 12 to 16 elephants, and has released three CDs. The elephants play simple woodwinds, harmonicas, a few string instruments and drums, although conductor Dave Soldier does say that some elephants have more musical talent than others.

Female elephants have a much larger vocabulary than the males, and the males can barely understand a word they say.

In fact, female elephants have stupendous vocabularies compared to the males, who are monosyllabic by comparison. This is because the males and females live very different lives: adult males are solitary; females live in big matriarch-led groups. One female call that male elephants can understand is the female invitation for sex. She emits this on just four days in four years, and though the call lasts only a few seconds, the male elephants can hear it over two miles away.

Prussian Field Marshal Blücher, the hero of Waterloo, confessed to the Duke of Wellington that he was pregnant, with an elephant, by a French grenadier.

Wellington's Prussian ally, who was 72 at Waterloo and only lived another four years after the battle, was a well-known nutcase. Some explain Blücher's insanity by the intensity of his dislike for the French, although the cause could equally have been his very heavy drinking, which might also have explained his renowned courage on the battlefield.

'They couldn't hit an elephant at this distance' were the last words of General John Sedgwick, Union Commander in the American Civil War, moments before he was killed by sniper fire.

Sedgwick's complacency got him killed at the beginning of the Battle of Spotsylvania Court House in 1864, while he was directing artillery placements. His remark was directed at artillerymen who ducked for cover at the sound of gunfire, just moments before he fell forward with a bullet hole beneath his left eye.

ELVIS PRESLEY

After Elvis's first appearance on stage, he was told that he would make a better lorry driver than singer.

Following his first appearance at the Grand Ole Opry in 1954, where he did not go down well with the regulars, one of the officials recommended he go back to driving a truck.

Elvis Presley referred to his manhood as 'Little Elvis'.

According to his biographer Albert Goldman, Elvis thought his uncircumcised penis was small and unattractive. 'Little Elvis' has now become a euphemism for a penis or a gun.

Tommy Steele gave Elvis a secret tour of London in 1958.

Contrary to popular belief, Elvis did visit England, and asked popular singer Steele to show him around, after first asking him, 'They tell me you're good. Are you as good as me?' However, the pair probably never left their car during the tour of the sights of the capital, for fear of being recognised and mobbed by fans.

Elvis Presley once presented President Nixon with a Colt 45 pistol.

In return, the singer asked if he could have a badge from the Bureau of Narcotics and Dangerous Drugs to add to his collection of police badges, a request that was granted. During the same secret visit to the White House in 1970, Elvis told Nixon that he thought the Beatles had been a real force for anti-American spirit, and assured the President that, when it came to drug culture and communist brainwashing, 'I'm on your side'.

1. GEORGE WASHINGTON
13th cousin 8 times removed
2. JOHN ADAMS
15th cousin 6 times removed
3. THOMAS JEFFERSON
13th cousin 8 times removed
4. JAMES MADISON
13th cousin 8 times removed
5. JAMES LAWRENCE MONROE
17th cousin 4 times removed
6. JOHN QUINCY ADAMS
15th cousin 6 times removed
7. ANDREW JACKSON
16th cousin 5 times removed
8. MARTIN VAN BUREN
25th cousin 3 times removed
9. WILLIAM HENRY HARRISON
5th cousin 5 times removed
10. JOHN TYLER
14th cousin 7 times removed
11. JAMES KNOX 'LITTLE HICKORY' POLK
19th cousin twice removed
12. ZACHARY TAYLOR
14th cousin 7 times removed
13. MILLARD FILLMORE
17th cousin 4 times removed
14. FRANKLIN PIERCE
22nd cousin 3 times removed
15. JAMES BUCHANAN
18th cousin 5 times removed
16. ABRAHAM LINCOLN
15th cousin 5 times removed
17. ANDREW JOHNSON
17th cousin 6 times removed
18. ULYSSES SIMPSON GRANT
19th cousin once removed
19. RUTHERFORD BIRCHARD HAYES
26th cousin twice removed
20. JAMES ABRAM GARFIELD
23rd cousin twice removed
21. CHESTER ALAN ARTHUR
Half 12th cousin 4 times removed
22. GROVER CLEVELAND
22nd & 24th President
19th cousin 4 times removed

23. BENJAMIN HARRISON
7th cousin 3 times removed
24. GROVER CLEVELAND
as 22
25. WILLIAM McKINLEY
16th cousin 7 times removed
26. THEODORE ROOSEVELT
18th cousin 3 times removed
27. WILLIAM HOWARD TAFT
17th cousin 5 times removed
28. THOMAS WOODROW WILSON
17th cousin 4 times removed
29. WARREN GAMALIEL HARDING
11th cousin 3 times removed
30. JOHN CALVIN COOLIDGE
20th cousin once removed
31. HERBERT CLARK HOOVER
19th cousin twice removed
32. FRANKLIN DELANO ROOSEVELT
19th cousin twice removed
33. HARRY S. TRUMAN
18th cousin 8 times removed
34. DWIGHT DAVID EISENHOWER
18th cousin 4 times removed
35. JOHN FITZGERALD KENNEDY
19th cousin twice removed
36. LYNDON BAINES JOHNSON
19th cousin once removed
37. RICHARD MILHOUS NIXON
20th cousin once removed
38. GERALD RANDOLPH FORD
19th cousin 4 times removed
39. JAMES EARL CARTER Jr.
24th cousin twice removed
40. RONALD WILSON REAGAN
17th cousin 4 times removed
41. GEORGE HERBERT WALKER BUSH
17th cousin 3 times removed
42. WILLIAM JEFFERSON BLYTHE CLINTON
25th cousin twice removed
43. GEORGE WALKER BUSH
18th cousin twice removed

Elvis is related to every American president except for Barack Obama.

George Washington and Thomas Jefferson are both 13th cousins eight times removed, Abraham Lincoln is his 15th cousin five times removed, Franklin D. Roosevelt his 19th cousin twice removed, and George W. Bush his 18th cousin twice removed. Oprah Winfrey claims Elvis is a distant cousin, but this has been disputed.

ENID BLYTON

Enid Blyton is widely reported to have enjoyed playing tennis in the nude.

Nude tennis was a common practice in those days among the more louche members of the middle classes.

Enid Blyton was banned by the BBC for nearly 30 years.

Blyton tried to get her work on the radio in 1940, but was turned down as, according to the BBC employee who read it, 'This is really not good enough. Very little happens and the dialogue is so stilted and long-winded . . . It really is odd to think that this woman is a bestseller.' In an internal memo dated 1938, Jean Sutcliffe, head of the BBC Schools Department, dismissed Blyton's work as lacking literary value, and it wasn't until 1963 that one of her pieces made it on to *Woman's Hour*.

Blyton fans can protect themselves against fires with a special edition Noddy smoke alarm.

The alarm, decorated with a smiling and calm-looking Noddy, is described as a collectable item on eBay.

Noddy is known as 'Oui Oui' in France.

Noddy has been published in 27 languages, and is known as 'Doddi' in Iceland, 'Hilitos' in Spain and 'Purzelknirps' in Germany.

Enid Blyton's successful titles include *Dame Slap and her School*, *Bimbo and Blackie Go Camping* and *Mr Pink-Whistle Interferes*.

Many of Blyton's titles sound dubious to present-day readers. Others include *Enid Blyton's Gay Story Book*, *Rubbalong Tales*, *Mr. Twiddle's Trumpet*, *Noddy Loses His Clothes*, *Noddy and the Magic Rubber* and *The Naughtiest Girl is a Monitor*.

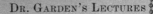
EYES

Where would we be without eyes? Well, obviously we wouldn't know where we were.

According to a recent survey carried out by De Montfort University, 8 per cent of A Level students think eyes are vegetables and grow in the garden like peas, and you get them out of eye-pods.

Although the ostrich is the third largest bird in the world, its brain is smaller than its eyeball, its stomach is smaller than its brain, its genitals are smaller than its stomach and its self-esteem is almost non-existent.

The early 3-D movie *House of Wax* was directed by Andre de Toth, who never appreciated the 3-D effect himself because he was blind in one eye, and deaf in the other.

The jelly-like content of the eye is greatly valued by butchers, who use it to fill up the space round the meat in pork pies.

In Kentucky the state flower is the bluebell, the state bird is the buzzard and the state body-part is the eye. As a result, Kentucky has more eye-related place names than any other state: over 500, including the towns of Squint, East and West Cornea, Retina Bluff and the Weeping Tears river.

People scoffed at pirates on the Spanish Main, who believed that piercing their ears and wearing an earring would improve their eyesight. In fact, the point on the lobe where the ear was pierced corresponds to the acupuncture point for the eyes. So now people scoff even louder.

In Germany, it was once believed that wearing the left eye of a bat as a talisman would make you invisible, and wearing both eyes of a bat would make you invisible to the bat.

Kiera Knightley was born with unnaturally hairy eyeballs, and still has to shave them three times a day. Hairy eyeballs affect one person in 900,000, whereas scaly eyeballs affect one person in Cardiff. The condition of having eyeball-hair is known as Optrichosis.

When the architect who designed St Basil's Cathedral in Red Square showed the half-finished building to Tsar Ivan the Terrible, he asked him, 'Do you want onions on that?' The Tsar thought he was joking, but when he saw the finished building and realised the architect actually *had* put onions on all the turrets, he had the poor man's eyes gouged out as punishment.

In China, members of the Ming dynasty were considered very ugly because of the shape of their eyes, which were round like a Westerners. Hence the verb – 'to ming': to look unattractive.

FACT ❶: The brain of the ostrich is smaller than its eyeball.

FACT ❷: The early 3-D movie House of Wax was directed by Andre de Toth, who never appreciated the 3-D effect himself because he was blind in one eye.

FACT ❸: Pirates believed that piercing their ears and wearing an earring would improve their eyesight. In fact, the point on the lobe where the ear was pierced corresponds to the acupuncture point for the eyes.

FACT ❹: In Germany, it was once believed that wearing the left eye of a bat as a talisman would make you invisible.

FACT ❺: When the architect who designed St Basil's Cathedral showed the half-finished building to Tsar Ivan, the Tsar had his eyes gouged out.

119

FINGERS

We have no muscles in our fingers.

Fingers have no long muscles, but move by the pull of forearm muscles on the tendons in the main part of the hand. However, fingers do contain thousands of very tiny 'muscle fibres', which cause hairs to stand up and blood vessels to contract.

Rolling Stones guitarist Keith Richards has had the middle finger of his left hand insured for £1 million.

He is not the only celebrity to have a body part insured; Dolly Parton has had each breast insured for $300,000, Jennifer Lopez has insured her bottom for $27 million, and Tom Jones's chest hair is insured for $7 million.

The Kentucky Fried Chicken slogan 'Finger-lickin' good' was mistranslated as 'Eat your fingers off' in Chinese.

KFC were one of the first Western companies to move in to China, establishing the first fast food restaurant in Mainland China in Beijing in 1987, within sight of Mao's mausoleum in Tiananmen Square.

The only character in *The Simpsons* with five fingers is God.

All other *Simpsons* characters, including Jesus, have only four fingers and toes.

Three-fingered Postman Pat was given an extra finger in Japanese merchandising, in case children thought he was a member of the Yakuza criminal society, whose members have their little fingers cut off to show loyalty.

More recently Bob the Builder's creators, Hit Entertainment, also decided to give all merchandising of three-fingered Bob an extra digit. Many Japanese believe the Western cartoon creators were being too sensitive, and while Japanese children might joke that the characters were in the mafia, they wouldn't be scared. 'Yubitsume', or finger shortening, is a Japanese ritual to atone for offences to another.

FLIES

1.
2.
4.
3.

Greek philosopher Aristotle refused to accept that flies had any more than four legs.

Aristotle's statement that flies only have four legs was repeated in books by naturalists for over 1,000 years, despite the fact that basic counting would have proved otherwise. Aristotle also maintained that men have more teeth than women – another error easily remedied had he bothered to count them.

One species of fruit fly produces sperm more than 20 times the length of its body.

To do this the tiny fruit fly 'Drosophila bifurca' has testicles that make up 11 per cent of their body weight, and the sperm are tightly coiled. If proportionate, the sperm of a man six feet tall would be 120 feet long.

Experts advise placing flypaper away from corners because flies prefer to breed in the centre of a room.

The many species of fly that mate 'on the wing' (while flying in circles) prefer mating in the centre of the room as it helps them avoid colliding with surfaces.

The coffin fly is able to live its entire life underground in a corpse, digging nearly a metre down through the soil to reach a buried coffin.

'Megaselia scalaris', also known as scuttle flies, can be recognised by their minute size, hump-back and jerky run. They are most active in a corpse that has been buried a year, after butyric fermentation has begun and the body is starting to dry, and they also thrive in mausoleums. Coffin flies dig through cracks in the soil, and several generations can occupy a corpse without coming to the surface.

In an effort to promote public hygiene, a Chinese city recently offered to buy dead flies from residents at the equivalent of 0.06 cents per fly.

Officials in the Xigong district of Luoyang city instigated the plan. According to Hi Guisheng, the district's administrative director, 'We think giving people money will be more effective than fining them to keep the city clean.'

FLORENCE NIGHTINGALE

Florence Nightingale pioneered and developed the first pie chart.

She was a passionate mathematician who produced 'the rose diagram', a prototype pie chart explaining the patterns of deaths from disease and combat in the Crimean War. She later became the first woman to be elected a fellow of the Royal Statistical Society.

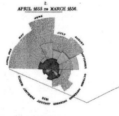

DIAGRAM of the CAUSES of MORTALITY
IN THE ARMY IN THE EAST.

Florence Nightingale owned a pet owl, which she carried around in her pocket.

Nightingale rescued her pet owl Athena from stone-throwing youths in Athens in 1850, and would tour the wards with it in her pocket. In 2009, the Florence Nightingale Museum in London launched a successful campaign to raise £13,000 to buy the stuffed animal, which they now have on display.

Florence Nightingale served only two years as a nurse.
She was an active nurse from 1851 to 1853, whilst training in Germany. Because of her background she was then appointed the superintendent of a women's hospital. And it was as a nursing manager, rather than as nursing staff, that she served in Crimea, supervising 38 nurses.

Florence Nightingale spent most of the last 53 years of her life in bed.
She was convinced she was suffering from terminal heart disease, although it is now thought these periods of being bed ridden were caused by a mixture of depression, chronic fatigue syndrome, and brucellosis, coupled with a concern to avoid the near helpless lives of her mother and older sister in Victorian society, despite their academic qualifications.

Florence Nightingale provided the world's first celebrity endorsement of a mail order business.
Sir Pryce Pryce-Jones set up the world's first mail-order drapery business, selling Welsh flannel by utilising the newly formed national postal service to send leaflets to customers. When he received an order from Florence Nightingale in 1862, he promptly began using her name in advertising material, without asking permission. Queen Victoria was also a customer, and he provided flannel as far afield as the United States and Australia.

FLOWERS

Cher has had several floral blooms tattooed on her buttocks.

The tattoos were applied by Bob Roberts of Sunset Tattoo in Los Angeles in 1972, and were revealed by many of her concert outfits in the 1980s.

The orchid is named after the Greek word for testicle, '*orchis*', due to the shape of its bulbous roots.

Before the name orchid came into common usage in Britain in 1845, the plant was referred to as a 'ballockwort'. An 'orchidometer' is the scientific instrument used for measuring the size of men's testicles.

Roses do not grow thorns; technically they have prickles.

Thorns grow from the wood of a plant, whereas prickles grow from the outer layer of the skin, and are therefore easier to break off.

On International Women's Day, Russian police stop women drivers in order to hand out flowers.

On 8 March, there is a growing tradition for Russian traffic police to present women drivers they pull over for minor traffic violations with flowers rather than tickets.

The Titan Arum or Corpse Flower of Sumatra is three metres tall and smells of dead flesh.

Fortunately, the plant rarely flowers, and only emits the nauseating stench when the flower is ready for pollination. Thought to have the largest flowering structure in the world, the plant also has a single, immense leaf, and tubers weighing 70 kg or more.

FOOTBALL

The Duke of Westminster had trials with Fulham, Angus Deayton had trials with Crystal Palace and Sir David Frost turned down a contract with Nottingham Forest.

Sadly, the Duke's father considered football an unseemly career for an aristocrat, and Sir David Frost turned down his contract in order to go to university. Other unlikely people to have had trials for football clubs include Des O'Connor for Northampton Town, and Bernard Manning and Eddie Large for Manchester City. Sir Arthur Conan Doyle, Albert Camus and Pope John Paul II were all keen goalkeepers.

Chelsea FC banned its fans from bringing celery to matches.

One of English football's stranger traditions is the Chelsea fans' ritual of pelting players with celery to the accompaniment of the 'Celery Song': 'Celery, celery, if she don't come, I'll tickle her bum, with a lump of celery'. In 2007, following a Carling Cup final during which Arsenal's Cesc Febregas was showered with celery while attempting to take a corner kick, Chelsea issued a statement: 'In future, if anyone is found attempting to bring celery into Stamford Bridge they could be refused entry and anyone caught throwing celery will face a ban.' In 1996, Second Division Gillingham was also forced to bring in a celery ban, after fans would regularly pelt their own goalkeeper, Jim Stannard, with sticks of the vegetable.

Before football referees started using whistles in 1878, they used to rely on waving a handkerchief.

The very first football players would call their own fouls, but officials were forced to bring in the handkerchief system as the game became more competitive. In American football officials still indicate that a foul has occurred by throwing a flag onto the field.

The Robot Soccer World Cup or 'RoboCup' is an international football competition involving teams of robot footballers from over 40 countries.

The RoboCup federation hope that 'by 2050, a team of fully autonomous humanoid robot soccer players will win a soccer game, complying with the official FIFA rules, against the winner of the most recent world cup of human soccer'.

One of the first English referees really was a 'Bastard'.

Segar Bastard was an English amateur football player and referee. He refereed the 1878 FA Cup Final between Wanderers and Royal Engineers at the Kennington Oval before refereeing the first ever England v. Wales match, at the Oval on 18 January 1879.

FOXES

The fox is the smallest member of the cat family. Since Neanderthal man first domesticated the fox it has been man's faithful companion.

The fox's tail or 'brush' is so called because in the Middle Ages the tail was used to clean the teeth. Fox droppings were known as 'toothpaste'.

Fox milk is a valuable source of aluminium. Children raised by wild foxes grow up to be completely rust-proof.

The Ancient Romans believed that you could cure a headache by tying the genitals of a fox to your forehead because, if nothing else, having a howling, snapping, angry fox attached to your head by its privates would probably take your mind off the headache.

Foxes are actually vegetarian. When a fox gets into a hen-house, the chickens go crazy and start tearing each other to shreds, despite the best efforts of fox to calm them down. This always gives farmers a good laugh.

On rainy days King Henry IV of France would move trees, rocks and grass into the Grande Galerie in the Louvre and stage indoor fox hunts down the middle of the corridor. Not to be outdone, King Henry VIII of England would put on full-scale indoor stag hunts in Hampton Court.

The foxtrot was invented in 1914 by Harry Fox from Charleston. The dance was banned in Japan where foxes are regarded as 'darkness devils' who whisper lethal spells into the ears of people as they sleep.

Incidentally, the Japanese for 'foxtrot' is '*fokkusu-torotto*'.

Her Majesty the Queen has a special hat made of fox fur. When she tells her husband that she is due to visit a place she has never heard of, Prince Philip will reply, 'Wear the fox hat'. This is believed to be a private joke.

The fox is famous for being trustworthy, honest, truthful and unbiased, which makes you wonder why Fox Television chose that name.

It takes at least 40 foxes to make a fur coat, although in Beijing it only takes two children to run one up.

Roadkill Recipes is Britain's first 'flattened fauna' cookbook by Arthur Boyt of Cornwall. As well as badger, weasel and bat there is a recipe for fox, although Boyt does say that fox tends to repeat on him. People with a sweet tooth might like to round off their meal with a Dessert Fox.

In the words of Oscar Wilde: 'The world may be divided into people that read, people that write, people that think and fox-hunters.'

FROGS

Auguste Escoffier first served frogs' legs in Britain as 'Cuisses de Nymphe a l'Aurore' or 'Thighs of the Dawn Nymphs'.

It was at a grande soirée in honour of the Prince of Wales at London's Savoy hotel in 1908 and it made frogs' legs the surprise culinary hit of the season. It's Escoffier who is credited with the introduction of frogs' legs to British menus.

The goliath frog from the African Congo can reach the size of a small terrier.

An endangered species, the goliath frog is the largest frog in the world.

One gram of poison from a Colombian kokoe poison arrow frog would be sufficient to kill up to 3,500 people.

One ounce of the poison from this bright yellow and black frog could kill around 100,000 average-sized men. Local people tip up to 50 arrows with poison by wiping the back of a single kokoi frog.

In Rangpur Province, Bangladesh, villagers perform mock weddings between frogs in the belief that the ritual will bring rain.

It's a centuries-old rain-making ritual that still continues to this day in times of drought. The frog bride and groom are highly decorated with a red streak of colour on their forehead and carried in a special basket to a banana-leaf stage. Villagers sing songs, make offerings of rice and grass, and then, after the ceremony, the married frogs are released into the village pond.

The paradoxical frog is considerably smaller as a frog than it is as a tadpole. And it grunts like a pig.

The South American paradoxical frog ('Pseudis paradoxa') grunts like a pig. It's paradoxical because the very large tadpoles – up to 25 cm long – are up to four times larger than the frog.

Giant tadpole
The tadpole of this frog grows to three times the size of the adult.

Model of paradoxical frog
Pseudis paradoxa
Trinidad and South America

FUNERALS

One-third of Taiwanese funeral processions include a stripper.

It remains common in rural areas to see funeral carts hauling flocks of scantily dressed girls from local nightclubs or brothels. In China, there is a strong and potent erotic undercurrent in funeral rituals, sometimes expressed through explicit language, erotic dance or even pornography. This is intended to incite sexual activity and the ensuing birth of offspring.

At funerals in Ancient China, mourners took a few steps back when the coffin lid was closed to ensure their shadows didn't get caught in the box.

Some people would even retreat to another room to avoid this danger to their health. When the coffin was lowered into the grave, people would stand on the side of the grave away from the sun, and the gravediggers tied their shadows to their waists with a strip of cloth.

The most common request made by Britons when planning their funeral is to be cremated with the ashes of their pet, closely followed by having a mobile phone in their coffin and for someone to ensure they are dead.

According to research conducted by Age Concern other common funeral requests are: 'to be buried in my own garden'; 'to be buried with all my savings'; and 'to be buried with my teeth in'. Age Concern do offer people the chance to be buried with their pets, but on the written proviso that: 'requests to be buried with one's pet's ashes are adhered to if the pet is already deceased'.

When Victor Hugo died, Parisian prostitutes wore black crepe around their private parts in a show of respect for one of their most illustrious clients.

The writer was a prominent figure in many parts of French society, and although a frequenter of brothels, was also a champion for social justice, famously stating that 'Slavery still exists, but now it applies only to women and its name is prostitution.' The government even gave Parisian prostitutes a grant to attend the funeral, so they wouldn't suffer a loss of income.

A Midlands church minister has adapted his Triumph motorbike so that it holds a sidecar big enough to carry a coffin.

The Reverend Paul Sinclair runs Motorcycle Funerals of Petersfield, and normally heads the funeral procession on the modified bike, which can reach speeds of 117.6 mph. He has even modified a tandem to carry a coffin at the request of a family of keen cyclists.

GAMBLING

The Romans played a form of strip poker.

One Roman glass painting depicts a young man and woman, both partially dressed with clothes strewn on the floor around them, seated at a tabula board, with an inscription reading 'Devincavi', meaning 'I think I've beaten you'. Tabula is a board game dating back several centuries BC, and is very similar to backgammon.

Russell Crowe worked as a bingo caller as a teenager.

He was fired from the job after using rude phrases to call numbers, including 'number one – up yer bum'. Crowe still enjoys playing bingo to relax, as do numerous other celebrities, including Bono and Robbie Williams.

There is a world poker championship for computers.

Since 2006, the Annual Computer Poker Competition has allowed computer programmers from all over the world to let their computers compete against each other over three variations of 'Texas Hold'em'. There are two winners in each event – the computer that wins most matches, and the computer that wins most money. Last year about 70 million hands were played in order to mediate the effects of luck and arrive at statistically significant results.

At Wimbledon in 1995, Ladbrokes took a £1,000 bet that Goran Ivanisevic would not smile on centre court.

The odds were good at 13/10, but Ivanisevic was so incensed when told about the bet that he smiled brightly for the cameras every time he appeared on court.

The Wynn hotel in Las Vegas has no fourth floor, for luck.

The number four is unlucky in Chinese culture because it is pronounced 'si', which is similar to the Chinese word for death. As Chinese punters are very important to the gambling industry in Vegas, several establishments avoid the number, including the Wynn and the Palazzo Resort Hotel Casino, which has no fourth, thirteenth or fourteenth floor. In China, people avoid having the number four at the start or end of phone numbers and number plates, and the fourth floors of new apartment buildings have the cheapest flats on them.

GEESE

Geese were trained to turn spits.

There are a number of 19th century accounts of geese being used for this tiring and uncomfortably hot job. The geese were either trained to turn the spits using their powerful necks like an arm, or were used in

wheels or treadmills connected to the spit. 'Turnspit dogs' were also used to turn such treadmills, but geese were able to keep spits turning for up to 12 hours at a time.

"The balance step without advancing."
Lord Haldane

The British Army were doing the goose step long before the Nazis.

It was known as the goose step in Britain as long ago as 1806, and was not used for ceremonial purposes but as a training step for new recruits to aid balance when marching. It is also thought that the Prussians might have been goose-stepping as far back as the 1600s.

Four jails in Brazil are using geese to help prevent prisoners from escaping.

The prisons, in São Paulo's Paraiba Valley, say no inmates have escaped since they brought in the geese. The geese are kept just inside the prison wall and make a lot of noise whenever anyone goes near them, as well as helping to alert guards to outbreaks of violence amongst rival gangs. Geese have long been used as guard animals, and legend has it that the Roman sacred geese in the temple of Juno saved Rome by alerting guards to invading Gauls with their loud honking.

In Ireland, geese were used to clean chimneys.

A large bird would be dropped down the flue from the roof, then pulled back up again by a rope attached to its neck. Its powerful wings would loosen the soot as it struggled – the blacker the bird, the cleaner the chimney. Ducks, chickens and turkeys were also used for this purpose.

If a goose is shot, its partner will return to stand vigil next to its corpse.

Geese show devotion to their dead partners, with hunters reporting seeing mates return to the spot where their partner was killed. Geese also do this if a mate dies of other causes, with a report from Canada describing how one goose stood vigil for six days after its mate had died on an ice floe, and even succeeded in scaring away an interested vulture. When a separated couple are reunited, especially when the male has scared off a predator, they will perform a 'triumph ceremony', which is a combination of dance and song, re-enacting their courtship.

A cross between a swan and a goose is called a 'swoose'.

Such hybrids don't usually survive past fledgling stage, although, in 2004 on the River Frome in Dorset a mute swan paired with a domestic goose and produced a single swoose which has survived to adulthood.

GERMANY

The garden gnome originated in Germany.

Garden gnomes as we know them today originated in Germany, as did the harmonica, the French poodle and cocaine. The first of these German gnomes to reach the UK were imported in 1847 by the eccentric spiritualist Sir Charles Isham, who brought a set of 21 back from Germany, using them to decorate a rockery at his estate at Lamport Hall in Northamptonshire. Isham's daughters, who disliked the gnomes, attempted to dispose of them, but missed one due to his having been well concealed in a garden crevice. The gnome that got away can be seen at Lamport Hall today and is known as "Lampy". Believed to be the oldest garden gnome in the world, Lampy is insured for £1 million.

German uniforms in the First World War were made of nettles.

During the war, the German empire, plagued by textile shortages, used nettles as a substitute for cotton. Captured German uniforms were found to be 85 per cent nettle fibre, which is very similar to hemp or flax. Nettle fibres were used extensively in the 17th century for making a range of cloths, from fine-textured fabrics to sailcloth and sacking.

Beer is officially classed as a food in Bavaria.

Technically, beer is always classed as a food as it provides nourishment, but in Bavaria it must also abide by the 'Reinheitsgebot', or purity law, which is thought to be the oldest food-quality regulation still in use today. Bavarian beer still adheres to the rules laid down in 1516 by William IV, Duke of Bavaria, which state that the only ingredients allowed are water, hops and barley-malt.

Friedrich Wilhelm I commissioned a regiment of giants.

William Frederick is said to have collected tall men for his army 'like stamps', establishing an elite regiment of outsized grenadiers that became known as the 'Potsdam Giants'. No member of the unit stood less than six feet tall, and many were closer to seven; the drill leader is said to have topped seven feet. One medical historian described them as 'the tallest men ever assembled until the birth of professional basketball'.

German submarine U-1206 was sunk by 'improper use' of the toilet by the captain.

U-1206, which went into service in March 1944, was one of the late war boats fitted with new deep-water high-pressure flushing toilets, which allowed them to be used at depth. Flushing these toilets was so complicated that special technicians were trained to operate them. On 14 April 1945, while off the coast of Scotland, official reports state that the captain's misuse flooded the submarine's batteries, releasing chlorine gas, and forcing the vessel to the surface, where it was bombed by British patrols. However, there has been speculation that this was a complicated surrender ploy from a captain who could see his side would soon lose the war.

GIRAFFES

The Camelopard.

The giraffe was originally called a 'camelopard' as it looks a bit like a camel and a bit like a leopard.

With the size and shape of a camel and the markings of a leopard, the animal's scientific classification is still *Giraffa camelopardalis*. The camelopard also appears in heraldry as a giraffe like animal with long, curved horns.

Same-sex relations amongst giraffes are more frequent than heterosexual behaviour.

Following aggressive 'necking', male giraffes frequently caress and court each other, leading up to mounting and climax. In one study, 94 per cent of observed mounting incidents took place between males, but only 1 per cent of same-sex mounting incidents occurred between females.

Homosexual behaviour has been observed in 1,500 species of animals, and is especially common amongst butterflies and manatees.

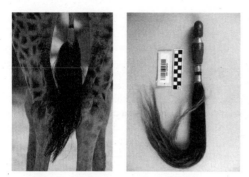

Giraffe tails are used as currency in some societies.

The tails have long been prized by many African cultures, and are used as unofficial currency in Uganda and Sudan. The tails can be used in good luck bracelets, fly whisks and thread, and their popularity has led people to kill a giraffe for the tail alone.

A giraffe's height is a constant danger to it in captivity. Of all the animals in the zoo, it's generally the giraffes that get struck by lightning.

This is especially true in wildlife parks, where the giraffe is often taller than surrounding buildings. Some scientists also think that the greater distance between the giraffe's legs makes it more likely for current to flow to the animal when lightning strikes.

A giraffe can clean its ears with its tongue.

The giraffe also uses its long prehensile tongue to clean its nostrils and eyes, as well as for grasping foliage. The 50 cm tongue is a purplish-black colour, which is thought to protect against sunburn.

GLUE

The glue on Israeli postage stamps is certified kosher.

This is also true of some Israeli children's glues, in case they eat them. In America, stamp 'gum' is both kosher and vegetarian – and once counted sweet potatoes and corn amongst its ingredients. There's only about one tenth of a calorie in the adhesive on the back of an American postage stamp, whereas British stamps contain 5.9 calories per lick as the glue is made from starch and polyvinyl alcohol. The adhesive on American lick-and-stick postage stamps is the only glue that needs to be approved by the US Food and Drug Administration.

Kevin Spacey glued his fingers together in the film _The Usual Suspects_ to give his left hand the feeling of paralysis.

In the 1995 film, Spacey also filed down his shoes to make them look more worn by his character's limp.

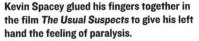

A Romanian father of five had to go to the doctors after he super-glued a condom to his penis.

In 2004, Nicolae Popovici told doctors at his local medical centre that he didn't want any more children, but unfortunately the 'super-size' condom he bought was too 'roomy' so he fixed it in place with glue. He also suggested that he hoped to reuse the condom.

'Geckel' is a new adhesive combining the sticky feet of geckos with the glue used by mussels.

The super-sticky material has been developed by scientists from Northwestern University in Illinois and can be used in both air and water. It is hoped that the material might have medical uses, as water-resistant adhesive for bandages and to replace sutures for wound closure.

Salvador Dali wore a homemade perfume made from artist's glue and cow dung.

In 1929, Dali began to display certain eccentric traits associated with mental illness, including suffering from uncontrollable fits of laughter, painting his armpits blue, wearing a red geranium over his ear and rubbing his body with a mixture of glue and cow or goat dung. This was also the time that Dali met Gala Diakonova, the love of his life, who, in spite of the perfume, became Dali's lover, model and muse, and provided a stabilising influence. Later in life, Dali lent his name to a perfume line from the Cofinluxe perfume house, for which he also designed a bottle, and the 'Salvador Dali' fragrance was launched in 1986, followed by 'Salvador Dali Pour Homme', 'Laguna', 'Dalimix', 'Daliflor', 'Rubylips' and 'Eau de Rubylips'.

GOLDFISH

Madame de Pompadour, mistress of Louis XV, was the first person in France to own a pet goldfish.

Her original name was Jeanne Antoinette Poisson, and the goldfish was imported from the Orient and presented as a curious gift to amuse her. However, the variety introduced to Europe at that time was the poorest and cheapest China had to offer.

Goldfish are susceptible to seasickness.

Dr Reinhold Hilbig, a zoologist from Stuttgart, found that many types of fish displayed signs of seasickness, including loss of balance, disorientation and nausea, when experiencing the effects of weightlessness. He believes this to be caused by loss of eye contact with water movement and vibrations.

Sticking things up goldfishes' noses will stop them breeding.

In 1976, researchers discovered that if you bung up a goldfish's nose so that it cannot smell, its sexual behaviour decreases significantly.

A goldfish will turn white if left for long enough in a darkened room.

Goldfish cells called chromataphores produce pigment in response to light, much like humans getting a suntan.

Goldfish have been taught to swim on their tails, as if standing up in the water.

In fact goldfish can be trained to perform many of the tricks dolphins are traditionally trained to perform – as is outlined in C. Scott Johnson's book *How To Train Goldfish Using Dolphin Training Techniques*. One goldfish in Pittsburgh, Pennsylvania, has been taught to swim through hoops and tunnels, push an underwater soccer ball into a goal, and fetch a ball from the bottom of the aquarium to the surface.

HOW TO TRAIN
—GOLDFISH—
USING
DOLPHIN TRAINING
TECHNIQUES

C. Scott Johnson

GOLF

Edward VII owned a golf bag made from an elephant's penis.

It was a gift from an Indian maharaja who had heard of the King's fondness for golf and big game hunting. Commentators have observed that since it would have been an Indian elephant, it's unlikely the King would have been able to get his full allocation of clubs into it; there would have been more room had it been an African elephant – as you can see from this photograph of a preserved African Elephant penis from Iceland's famous Penis Museum.

Before 1850, golf balls were made of leather and stuffed with feathers.

This type of golf ball, known as a 'featherie', was introduced in 1618. As it was individually handcrafted, it meant the ball was priced beyond the means of the masses, and sometimes cost more than a club.

Tiger Woods' first televised game of golf was at the age of two.

It was on *The Mike Douglas Show* in the US. The footage shows a two-year-old Tiger hitting a shot to the delight of the audience and guest Bob Hope.

Rudyard Kipling invented the game of snow golf, painting his balls red so they could be seen in the snow.

According to the United States Golf Association, Kipling invented the game in Vermont where he lived for four years. It is said that when visiting from Britain, Kipling's friend Sir Arthur Conan Doyle brought him a pair of skis and introduced the sport of skiing to Vermont.

There are two golf balls on the moon.

Both were hit by astronaut Alan Shepard on 6 February 1971. Shepard didn't play them where they lay and didn't have a caddy to retrieve them. He mishit the first, which went only about 100 feet, but the second stayed in the air for 30 seconds and went 200 yards.

HAIRDRESSERS

Hairdressing is the fourth most popular career choice for girls in the UK, after lacrosse coach, network systems analyst and construction worker. Among the famous who have started their working lives as hairdressers are Kenneth Williams, Martin Shaw, Janet Street-Porter and Yul Brynner, who interestingly was also a lacrosse coach.

Russia has always been the world leader in terms of hairdressing and hairstyle. Catherine the Great of Russia was so determined that the discovery of dandruff on her collar should be kept a secret, she locked her hairdresser in an iron cage for three years to stop the news spreading. Queen Victoria on the other hand was completely bald, and had a series of wigs made up for her by the Royal Wigmakers: Forsyth and Windsor.

In England under Cromwell and the Puritans, the elaborate hairstyles favoured by the Royalists were outlawed. Everyone's hair was shaved short by teams of Welsh hill farmers, used to shearing sheep. The affectionate term for these haircutters was 'Baa-Baa' which later became the more familiar 'Barber', and everyone knows that the red and white striped pole still seen on many a high street originally indicated a Hong Kong brothel.

In most ladies salons, when a hairdresser finds lice in a customer's hair, he or she will immediately start chatting about the weather as a coded sign to the other hairdressers to keep clear.

All salons now have a delousing fumigation chamber in the back for the use of staff. The New Zealand huhu beetle, known as the haircutter, has sharp hooks on its long legs, so if one lands in your hair and gets entangled you need a haircut to get it out.

Modern hairdressing really began with Siegfried Sassoon, who learned his trade in the trenches of the First World War, styling the long hair of the officers who entertained the troops with female impersonations.

It's often said that women are more faithful to their hairdressers than they are to their chiropodists. During the World Cup 2006, Wayne Rooney's girlfriend Coleen McLoughlin made a 900-mile round trip from Germany to Liverpool – to visit her favourite hairdresser.

In the United States, hairdressers are more strictly regulated than doctors, and the exams are more rigorous. A law in Illinois prohibits barbers from using their fingers to apply shaving cream to a customer's face, and in Missouri, men are only allowed to style ladies' hair if they keep at least one foot on the ground.

FACT ⊗ : A law in Illinois prohibits barbers from using their fingers to apply shaving cream to a customer's face.

FACT ⊗ : During the World Cup 2006, Wayne Rooney's girlfriend Coleen McLoughlin made a 900-mile round trip from Germany to Liverpool – to visit her favourite hairdresser.

FACT ⊗ : The New Zealand huhu beetle, known as the haircutter, has sharp hooks on its long legs, so if one lands in your hair and gets entangled you need a haircut to get it out.

FACT ⊗ : The red and white striped pole indicated a Hong Kong brothel.

FACT ⊗ : Catherine the Great of Russia was so determined that the discovery of dandruff on her collar should be kept a secret, she locked her hairdresser in an iron cage for three years to stop the news spreading.

151

HAMBURGERS

In Oklahoma, it is illegal to take a bite out of someone else's hamburger.

It is also illegal to make an ugly face at a dog, to wear your boots to bed, or to go whaling in the land-locked state. However, a law banning tattoos was repealed in 2006.

By weight, hamburgers cost more than new cars.

A Burger King Whopper costs £13,782 per tonne, whereas a Renault Clio costs just £11,234 per tonne. Additionally, producing a half-pound hamburger releases as much CO_2 into the atmosphere as driving a 3,000-pound car nearly ten miles.

A Swiss firm has invented a cheeseburger in a can.

The burger is meant for trekkers to eat in the wilderness, and is intended to be heated in a water container over fire for just two minutes before it is ready to eat. The burger has a shelf life of a year and is lightweight to carry. The same company also makes a travel chocolate mousse and a glass of red wine in a bag.

 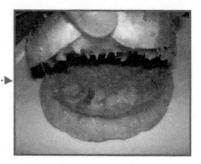

McDonald's employees can receive training at the officially accredited Hamburger University.

Fred Turner, McDonalds former senior chairman, founded the university in the basement of a McDonalds restaurant in Elk Grove Village, Illinois, in 1961. Today, more than 5,000 students attend Hamburger University in Illinois each year and there are campuses in London, Sydney, Munich, São Paulo and Shanghai. Courses include grill cleaning and burger flipping.

The founder of the McDonald's hamburger chain is a Bachelor of Hamburgerology (BH).

Ray Kroc, the man who made McDonalds a global franchising chain, has completed the training at Hamburger University and awarded the qualification to himself.

HATS

Top hats were originally thought to be deeply offensive and it's said that the first wearer of the top hat was arrested and charged £50 for disturbing the peace.

In the 1790s John Hetherington, a hatter in Charing Cross, was the first person to make a top hat and wear it in the street. It's reported that the sight of it caused a commotion among passers-by. Hetherington was booed and jeered, several women fainted, and a small boy broke his arm. Hetherington even ended up in court, and was fined £50 for: 'appearing on the public highway wearing upon his head a tall structure having a shining lustre and calculated to frighten timid people'.

The first stethoscopes were carried under doctors' top hats.

The instrument for listening to the heart was invented in 1816, at the same time top hats were becoming fashionable. Early stethoscopes were hollow wooden tubes, and some came with removable shafts so they would fit in the hat. Later, sectioned stethoscopes were developed to make them easier to fit under a hat or in a pocket.

The top hat was originally developed as a crash helmet.

The hat was intended to be worn when riding, in particular to protect the fox hunter from possible concussion if he fell from his horse in the course of the hunt. John Hetherington adapted his invention of the top hat from the riding hat. An inner band on the hat contained a drawstring that was tightened to hold the hat on the wearer's head, even when jumping over fences.

The Panama hat doesn't come from Panama.

It actually comes from Ecuador. It gets its name because goods in South America usually went through Panama before being exported to the rest of the world. It's like Stilton cheese, which takes its name from the village of Stilton in Cambridgeshire where the cheese was first sold at the Bell Inn, but was actually made in Leicestershire. Today it's actually illegal to make Stilton cheese in Stilton.

Sometimes Prince Philip hides a radio in his top hat when he attends Ascot races.

Unlike his horse-loving wife, the Prince dislikes racing and much prefers to listen to the cricket under his hat.

HENRY FORD

Henry Ford kept Thomas Edison's last breath in a test tube.

Henry Ford considered Thomas Edison his personal hero, and requested the test tube from Edison's son Charles. Ford had an interest in reincarnation, and was said to believe that the soul exited the body through the last breath. The test tube can be seen today in the Henry Ford Museum.

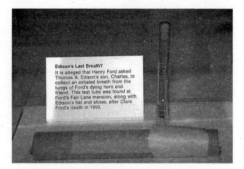

Edison's Last Breath?
It is alleged that Henry Ford asked Thomas A. Edison's son, Charles, to collect an exhaled breath from the lungs of Ford's dying hero and friend. This test tube was found at Ford's Fair Lane mansion, along with Edison's hat and shoes, after Clara Ford's death in 1950.

At the 1934 world's fair in New York City, Henry Ford served a 16-course meal – including soup, 'meat', vegetables, dessert, 'milk' and 'coffee' – all made from soya beans.

He also ordered many Ford auto parts to be made from soy-derived plastic, and once appeared at a convention with his entire attire, except for his shoes, having been produced from soybeans.

Henry Ford believed that cows were inefficient and unsanitary, proposing instead that milk should be made synthetically.

In 1921, Henry Ford declared that 'the cow must go'. It is thought that his hostile attitude to the animal may have stemmed from unpleasant experiences on his father's farm as a child.

Outlaw Clyde Barrow of Bonnie & Clyde fame once wrote a fan letter to Henry Ford.

The letter read, 'I have drove Fords exclusively when I could get away with one. It has every other car skinned, and even if my business hasn't been strictly legal it don't hurt anything to tell you what a fine car you got in the V-8.' A month later, he and partner Bonnie Parker were shot dead in a stolen Ford V-8.

Hitler was a great admirer of Henry Ford and kept a framed photo of him in his office.

The feeling was mutual, and Ford also kept a framed photograph of Hitler on his desk in Dearborn, Michigan and was a generous contributor to the Nazi movement. Ford is the only American referred to in *Mein Kampf* and was awarded a medal, the Grand Cross of the German Eagle, for his support for the Nazi Party. Henry Ford's factories in Germany contributed significantly to the build-up of the country's armed forces prior to World War II. During a strike at Ford's River Rouge Plant in 1941, pickets and their children held up signs comparing Henry Ford and Hitler.

HONEY

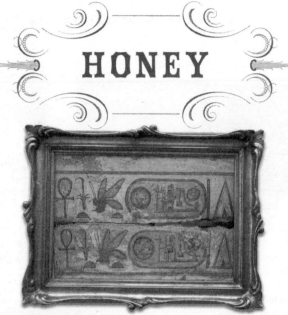

Honey is the only food that never goes off.

Honey found in the tombs of Egyptian pharaohs has been tasted by archaeologists and found to be edible. This is because honey has a low pH, contains a number of antibacterial properties, and is hydroscopic, meaning that it won't spoil providing the moisture content remains below 17 per cent.

King Pepi II of Egypt would smear naked slaves with honey to form 'human flypaper'.

Flies would swarm towards the honey, and leave the king in peace. Pepi II came to the throne aged six, and his reign is said to have lasted between 64 and 94 years. Only two statues of Pepi II have ever been found, both depicting him as a boy king.

Alexander the Great was coated in honey after death.

This was to preserve his body, as was the general practice, according to chroniclers of the time. Honey is effective as an embalming procedure due to its ability to extract moisture from its surroundings.

One favoured form of Persian execution involved the condemned person being stripped naked, covered with honey, trapped like a walnut between two narrow rowing boats, and left to the mercy of biting insects on a stagnant pond.

Called 'scaphism' or 'the boats', it was designed to inflict a particularly torturous death.

Out of 20,000 species of bees, only seven make honey.

To make one kilogram of honey, honey bees have to visit four million flowers, travelling a distance equal to four times around the earth.

HORSES

A horse shampoo called Lucky Kentucky was considered so good on human hair, it sold more than 900,000 bottles in Japan in 1997.
The shampoo is particularly suited to dark, straight hair, and is sold in bottles advertising it 'for mane, hair and body'. Lucky Kentucky also export a hoof and nail moisturising cream, intended to prevent hooves splitting when horses are shod, which has proved popular for use on human nails.

A zebra crossed with a horse is a 'zorse'.
The generic term for any equine–zebra cross is a 'zebroid', and there are sub-classes for specific animals, such as 'zeedonk', a cross between a zebra and a donkey. Zorses look more like horses than zebras, but have stripes and are resistant to certain horse diseases.

Clint Eastwood is allergic to horses.

Despite having appeared in over 20 westerns, Clint Eastwood revealed to the *New York Daily News* in 2008 that horses make him sneeze. It seems he isn't fond of the animals either, advising that: 'when you're around an animal that weighs 1,200 to 1,300 pounds and has the brain of a walnut, you've got to be on your best behaviour'.

The racehorse name 'Hoof Hearted' managed to make it past the American Jockey Club censor.

Other rude-sounding names that also made it past include 'Peony's Envy', 'Sofa Can Fast' and 'Alpha Kenny Won'. In 2003 Wayne Rooney tried to get the names 'Hoof Hearted' and 'Norfolk Enchants' past the censors of the British Racing Authority, but they were rejected.

The long jump for horses used to be an Olympic event.

This event was only ever contested once, at the 1900 Paris Olympics, where the jumps turned out to be disappointingly modest in comparison to human long jumps. A horse called 'Extra Dry' won the event with a jump of 20 feet and a quarter of an inch, which is 8 feet 7 $^1/_2$ inches less than the current human world record.

Extra-Dry, à M. Van Langhendonck, officier de guides belges, gagnant du saut en longueur, sautant 6 m. 10.

HOTELS

David and Jean Davidson lived in a Travelodge for 22 years.

The couple stayed at Travelodges in Newark and Grantham between 1985 and 2007, finding it a comfortable and cheaper alternative to an old people's home. They spent £97,600 on their hotel costs, whereas 'Help the Aged' say the cost of a residential care home for one person is between £21,000 and £25,000 a year. Mr Davidson said: 'We don't get hit with huge heating bills over the winter and it's safer than a lot of places these days. We get great rates because we book well in advance and all our bed linen is laundered too. It doesn't get much better than that, does it? We only have to walk across the car park for meals as there is a Little Chef here too.'

The Daspark Hotel is made from sections of concrete pipes, each with a double bed squashed inside.

Founded by Andreas Strauss in 2004, there are now two Daspark Hotel sites in Austria and Germany, consisting of concrete pipes containing beds, blankets and electrical sockets. They have also had their walls painted to make them 'a little more user friendly'.

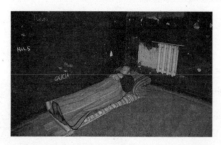

A hotel in Latvia offers guests the experience of living in a Soviet prison.

In Liepaja, Latvia, the old Karosta jail has been converted into a hotel, but the experience for the visitor remains much the same as in its previous incarnation. After check in, residents are handcuffed, stripped of belongings and ordered to scrub out toilets before being fed bread and water and sleeping on hard wooden floorboards in damp cells.

Staff in Japanese hotels are trained to bow with the help of an automated bowing machine.

Department store manager Chiyuki Takaishi invented the machine in the 1980s, after lamenting the decline in bowing skills, which he blames on the breakup of the traditional family. The contraption works by manipulating metal plates locked to the learner's body, familiarising them with the correct angles of bowing.

There is a hotel shaped like a crocodile in the Australian outback near Ayers Rock.

The Gagudju Crocodile Holiday Inn was designed in conjunction with local aboriginal people to look like a 250-metre crocodile. Guests enter through the jaws, and a swimming pool is positioned to represent the animal's heart.

ICE CREAM

In Japan you can buy an ice cream called 'Basashi' made from raw, minced horse flesh.

Shop-bought Basashi ice cream contains chunks of raw horseflesh. Other Japanese ice cream flavours include octopus and squid ink. Chicken wing ice cream is a regional speciality of Nagoya, a city famous for its poultry.

Ice cream sundaes were invented as a result of a religious ban that did not allow the sale of soda on Sundays.

In the late 19th century, there was a concentrated effort by Midwestern religious leaders against the sale of 'sucking sodas' on the Sabbath, prompting the invention of the 'ice cream sundae', which got round the ban by replacing the soda with syrup and candied cherry.

Margaret Thatcher helped develop the process by which Mr Whippy ice cream is made.

The chemistry graduate worked for a research team that discovered a method of doubling the amount of air in ice cream, which allowed manufacturers to use less of the actual ingredients, thereby reducing costs.

During the Second World War, the US Navy commissioned the world's first floating ice cream parlour for service in the Pacific.

The 'Ice Cream Barge' was commissioned in 1945 at a cost of around $1 million. Its sole purpose was to provide ice cream to sailors in the Pacific, and to this end the concrete barge was capable of producing 10 gallons every seven seconds.

It is illegal to buy ice cream after 6pm in Newark, New Jersey, unless you have a written note from a doctor.

In Kansas, it is illegal for eateries to serve ice cream on cherry pie, and it is illegal to walk around with an ice cream cone in your pocket on a Sunday in both New York and Kentucky.

ISAAC NEWTON

When Isaac Newton was a little baby he never slept at all until the age of five. To solve the problem his mother hung six steel balls above Newton's cradle and set them in motion, hoping it would help him to sleep. It worked because inevitably one of the steel balls would hit him on the head.

Isaac Newton always wanted to be a ballet dancer but he dropped out of school early because his mother wanted him to be a farmer.

After spending many happy years farming aubergines just outside Clitheroe, Newton started a brewery with his neighbour Josiah Ridley, and indeed Newton and Ridley beers are still popular in the north of England to this day.

One day he saw an apple fall from a tree and it set him wondering about the force acting upon it. Once he had invented gravity, Newton made his fortune by patenting it and only allowing

people to use it under licence. Once the gravity market had collapsed under its own weight, Newton turned his mind in other directions and he is now largely remembered for his many inventions. Among the devices he developed are the helicopter, the digital watch, the after-dinner mint and the cat-flap.

After being fired by Oxford University, Newton returned to the farm. There he spent the long winter evenings inventing optics – hailed as a great boon to the pub industry. One day he saw a rainbow fall out of a tree, and it set him wondering how light was made up. As it happens, Newton only identified six colours in the light spectrum. However 'seven' was his lucky number, so he added another one for luck: indigo, even though it isn't really a proper, separate colour.

Newton sadly failed to patent 'light' – he was beaten to it by young Thomas Edison. So he returned to his farm. One day he saw a pocket calculator fall out of a tree and it set him wondering what kind of a tree that was. But not being a biologist, he couldn't be bothered to find out.

Newton's other careers outside the world of science were all dismal failures. His first and only reported speech in the House of Commons as a Member of Parliament was to ask someone to close the window.

This just in from the US: in the town of Isaac Newton, Ohio, it is illegal to sell apples as souvenirs.

FACT ❶ : He dropped out of school early because his mother wanted him to be a farmer.

FACT ❻ : He saw an apple fall from a tree and it set him wondering about the force acting upon it.

FACT ❷ : Among the devices he developed is the cat-flap.

FACT ❸ : Newton only identified six colours in the light spectrum. However 'seven' was his lucky number, so he added another one for luck; Indigo, even though it isn't really a proper, separate colour.

FACT ❹ : His first and only reported speech in the House of Commons as a Member of Parliament was to ask someone to close the window.

167

JAMES BOND

James Bond is known as 'Mr Kiss Kiss, Bang Bang' in Italy.

The original main title theme to *Thunderball* was entitled 'Mr Kiss Kiss, Bang Bang', written by John Barry and Leslie Bricusse. The title was taken from an Italian journalist who in 1962 dubbed agent 007 as 'Mr Kiss Kiss, Bang Bang'.

The name of the Bond villain, Blofeld, was inspired by the father of the English cricket commentator, Henry Blofeld.

Fleming knew Blofeld as they went to Eton together. He often used the names of people he knew, including 'Scaramanga', named after George Scaramanga with whom he was also at school, and 'Goldfinger', named after architect Erno Goldfinger.

James Bond grew up in a place called Pett Bottom.

Bond's obituary in *You Only Live Twice* reveals that he grew up with his aunt in Pett Bottom, a real settlement five miles south of Canterbury. Fleming wrote much of *You Only Live Twice* in a pub called The Duck Inn in Pett Bottom.

Explorer Sir Ranulph Fiennes auditioned for the role of James Bond.

Despite having little acting experience, Sir Ranulph got through to the last six to play Bond after Sean Connery quit, but producer Cubby Broccoli said his hands were too big and he had a face like a farmer.

There is a church in Toronto, Canada, called the St James-Bond United Church.

When Ian Fleming was a Naval Intelligence Commander during the Second World War, he was billeted at a private house on Avenue Road in Toronto close to the St James-Bond United Church. When Fleming later conceived the character of Bond, it's suggested that the primary source for the name was the author of a favourite book: *Field Guide to Birds of the West Indies* by the American ornithologist James Bond. Could this church have already located the name James Bond in Fleming's subconscious?

169

JOSEPH STALIN

A company has developed a war strategy computer game called 'Stalin vs Martians'.

In the game the player must command Stalin and his Red Army to defend Russia against a fictional alien attack in 1942. *Gamespot* magazine awarded the game 1.5 out of 10, calling it: 'perhaps the worst real-time strategy game ever created'.

In 1906 Stalin temporarily resigned from the communist party over its ban on bank robberies.

He did this so he could rob the Imperial Bank in Tiflis, which he did on 26 June 1907, with guns and home-made bombs. Around 40 people were killed, and Stalin's gang made off with 250,000 roubles, approximately $3.4 million in today's money.

Stalin's only regular job was as a weatherman.

At the age of 21, Stalin became a weatherman at the Tiflis Meteorological Observatory, observing and recording meteorological data. Before this, he had been training to become a priest.

There's an amusement park in Lithuania known as Stalin's World.

The park's official title is Grutas Park and it's a sculpture garden of Soviet-era statues of the USSR's most brutal dictators, and re-creations of Soviet gulag prison camps, including wooden paths, barbed-wire fences and guard towers playing communist marches. However, a plan by its creator to transport visitors in a gulag-style train was not allowed.

Stalin had webbed toes on his left foot.

According to Simon Sebag Montefiore's book *Young Stalin*: 'despite his webbed toes, pockmarked face, and one useless arm, he was a magnet for women'. Other famous webbed footers include Dan Aykroyd and Ashton Kutcher.

JULIUS CAESAR

Julius Caesar wore a laurel wreath most of the time to hide his baldness.

The ruler's baldness was ironic since the family name Caesar means 'hairy'. According to Roman historian Suetonius, 'Julius Caesar kept his body carefully trimmed and shaved, his superfluous hair plucked, his bald spot combed over and covered by his laurel wreath.' Caesar wasn't the only vain, bald leader: Hannibal wore a wig into battle.

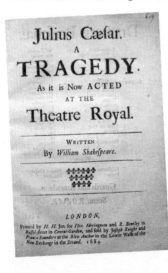

Julius Cæsar.
A
TRAGEDY.
As it is Now ACTED
AT THE
Theatre Royal.

WRITTEN
By *William Shakespeare.*

LONDON,
Printed by *H. H.* Jun. for *Hen. Heringman* and *R. Bentley* in *Russel-street* in *Covent-Garden,* and sold by *Joseph Knight* and *Francis Saunders* at the *Blew Anchor* in the Lower Walk of the *New Exchange* in the *Strand.* 1684.

The first recorded use of the phrases 'Right on' and 'It's all Greek to me' were in Shakespeare's *Julius Caesar.*

The 1599 play sees Mark Antony declaring that: 'To stir men's blood: I only speak right on', and Casca complains that he cannot understand Cicero's Greek.

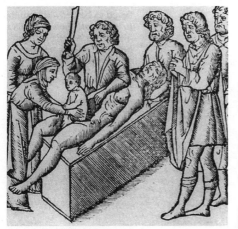

Julius Caesar was supposed to have been delivered by Caesarean section.

However, the operation is not named after his birth in 100 BC, but comes from the Latin 'caesus', the past participle of the verb 'to cut'.

In a pack of playing cards, the King of Diamonds represents Julius Caesar.

Each king in a deck of playing cards represents a great king from history. The King of Spades is King David; the King of Clubs is Alexander the Great; and the King of Hearts is Charlemagne.

Until it was renamed after Julius Caesar, the month of July was called Quintilis.

The month was renamed by the Roman Senate in honour of the Roman general, as July was the month of his birth.

KISSING

Some cultures kiss by biting off one another's eyelashes.

In many Pacific islands, there is no concept of erotic kissing, but biting is considered erotic. Inhabitants of the Trobriand Islands 'kiss' in a three-step procedure, beginning with biting each other's lower lips, then pulling their partner's hair, before nibbling off each other's eyelashes. As a result, it is a status symbol to have short eyelashes, as it is a sign of your popularity.

The Romans had different terms to classify different kisses.

'Osculum' was a peck on the cheek, 'basium' a more amorous kiss, and a Roman snog was called a 'saviolum'. Ancient Romans provide

some of the earliest records of kissing in the Western world, and used kisses in all walks of life, from greeting friends to showing respect for rulers.

North American porcupines kiss each other on the lips.
It's a kiss that actually involves the male and female rubbing noses as part of the mating ritual, but in the process, their lips do appear to touch.

Kissing helps reduce tooth decay.
This is because kissing increases saliva flow, which washes out the mouth and helps remove food particles, much like brushing. The mineral ions found in saliva can even promote the repair of small lesions in tooth enamel, although for those without a kissing partner, chewing gum has much the same effect.

In the 19th century, women travelling alone on trains used to place pins between their lips when entering tunnels.
Victorian guidebooks advised this as a method for women to ward off strange men who might try to kiss them in the dark.

LEMONS

In the Middle Ages, it was believed that lemon should be served with fish as it would prevent the diner from choking on bones.

The custom of serving a slice of lemon with fish dates from this time, when it was believed that the acidic lemon juice could dissolve an accidentally swallowed fish bone. Other citrus fruits and sorrel were also added to food for the same reason.

At the Battle of Lepanto in 1571, oranges and lemons were used instead of ammunition.

When the outnumbered Ottoman fleet ran out of missiles they threw lemons and oranges at the Holy League soldiers, who in turn threw them back, prompting scenes of hysterical laughter amid the carnage of the naval battle, during which it is estimated that, adrift in a sea jammed solid with corpses, 40,000 men died in just four hours. It was a rate of slaughter unsurpassed till the First World War.

Casanova would give his mistresses partially squeezed lemon halves to use as contraceptives.

The celebrated Italian gambler and lover was an advocate of the idea of 'barrier contraception', and wrote about it in volume eight of *Histoire de ma Vie*, his 12-volume memoirs. The idea was that the lemon shell acted as a physical barrier, and the juice as an acidic spermicide.

Rubbing a lemon under your arms is a traditional Puerto Rican treatment for a hangover.

Limes are also used for this purpose, as it is incorrectly believed that citrus fruit prevents sweating and so helps the body retain fluids and prevents headaches. In Romania, boiled tripe is believed to counter the effects of a hangover, and in Outer Mongolia pickled sheep's eyes in tomato juice are the preferred hangover cure.

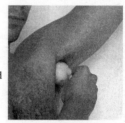

The drinking straw was designed to have a diameter just narrow enough to prevent lemon pips being sucked up.

When Marvin Stone invented the drinking straw in 1888, he also decided the ideal straw length was 8 $^{1}/_{2}$ inches. Before Stone's invention, beverage drinkers used natural rye grass straws.

LEONARDO DA VINCI

An Etch-a-Sketch version of the 'Mona Lisa' has been valued at $10,000.

American Jeff Gagliardi is one of a number of artists who have used the limitations of the toy to produce pop art, some of which has even attracted the attention of US presidents.

Leonardo was famous in his time for having uncommon physical strength and was proud of his ability to manipulate metal with his bare hands.

Vasari's *Lives of the Artists* reports: 'He could twist horseshoes between his fingers, bend bars of iron across his knees, disarm every adversary, and in wrestling, running, vaulting, and swimming he had no equals.'

Leonardo invented an alarm clock that woke the sleeper up by gently raising his feet.

The contraption used a thin stream of water dripping from one container to another over an allotted time. Once the second container filled, the legs of the sleeper were lifted by pulleys, waking him up.

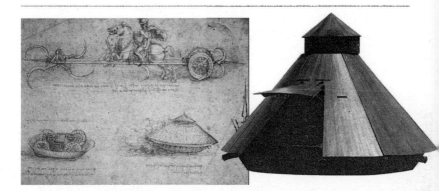

Leonardo Da Vinci designed the first tank.

His sketchbooks from 1487 reveal the blueprint for a crank-handle-powered tank, and in a letter to his patron, Ludovico Sforza, he reports: 'I can make armoured cars, safe and unassailable, which will enter the close ranks of the enemy with their artillery, and no company of soldiers is so great that it will not break through them.'

Leonardo suggested that the beaver, aware that humans harvested its testicles for medicinal properties, would deliberately chew them off as a life-saving measure.

This was a widely held belief that Leonardo had read, suggesting that the beaver does so to be at peace with its pursuers by leaving the testicles for them to collect. Medieval illuminations such as the one here show the beaver doing exactly this.

LEWIS CARROLL

It's widely believed that Queen Victoria enjoyed reading *Alice's Adventures in Wonderland* so much that she requested Carroll send her a copy of his next book, which, much to her disappointment, turned out to be about algebra.

An Oxford maths tutor, Carroll published nearly a dozen books on the subjects of geometry, matrix algebra, mathematical logic and recreational mathematics under his real name Charles Dodgson. On receiving the request it's said he couldn't resist sending the Queen a copy of his next work, *An Elementary Treatise On Determinants, With Their Application To Simultaneous Linear Equations And Algebraical Geometry*, published in 1867.

Lewis Carroll wrote most of his books standing up.

Lewis Carroll generally preferred to be on his feet, and preferably moving; when making tea for friends, he would walk up and down the room, waving the teapot and telling anecdotes. During the 18th and 19th centuries, standing desks were popular in both homes and offices, and the Prime Minister Lord Palmerston worked standing up in order to keep himself awake during long days.

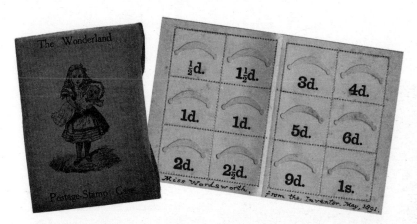

Lewis Carroll devised a system for writing in the dark called the 'nyctograph', and to promote letter writing, 'The Wonderland Postage Stamp-Case'.

Carroll also invented a system of mnemonics for remembering names and dates, and 'improved' the game of backgammon.

Lewis Carroll invented the word 'chortle'.

'Chortle' originated as a nonsense word in *Alice Through The Looking Glass*, meaning a combination of chuckle and snort. Carroll referred to such combination words as 'portmanteau words' due to their resemblance of the bag, which has two equal compartments that fasten together in the middle.

Lewis Carroll never wore an overcoat.

Lewis Carroll's biographer Collingwood reports that he never wore an overcoat, and that he died aged 65 of pneumonia. According to Collingwood, Carroll had a variety of eccentric preferences, including always wearing a tall hat and eating nothing for lunch but a glass of wine and a biscuit.

LIONS

Giraffe kicks have been known to decapitate lions.

This defence tactic has been witnessed by Kenyan park officials. An ostrich can also kill a lion with a powerful kick from one of its two-toed feet, each equipped with a long, sharp claw.

Lions' testicles are considered an aphrodisiac.

In Georgian times, lions were hunted for their testicles, which were believed to improve sexual performance. There are still African tribes today that consider this to be so, and they hunt lions specifically for the purpose of harvesting the testicles, before drying them, and grinding them into a powder prior to consumption. Goats and bulls' testicles are also considered aphrodisiacs in various parts of the world. The South African expression "to play with a lion's testicles" means "to take foolhardy chances".

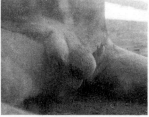

A lion's life expectancy is lower than that of the zebra it chases.

In the wild, lions rarely live past 10 due to injuries sustained from continual fighting with rival males, although lionesses live longer – usually 15–18 years. In comparison, zebra have an average lifespan in the wild of 25 years.

During the reign of Kublai Khan, the Chinese used lions on hunting expeditions.

The lions were trained to act like hunting dogs, and would drag down large prey, like wild bulls and bears, and stay with the kill until the hunting party arrived. Kublai Khan also had hunting leopards for his huge hunting park in Shangdu, and Marco Polo reported that the big cats were housed indoors with companion dogs when not hunting, in order to keep them calm.

King George III kept a quartet of lions at the Tower of London, called Fanny, Miss Fanny, Miss Howe and Miss Fanny Howe.

The animals are described in the 1800 guide to the Tower, and the Howes were named after Admiral Howe, since they were born on 1 June 1794, the day after his great victory over the French.

LOBSTERS

The verb 'to lobby' takes its meaning from the practice of trying to influence an MP by treating him to a champagne and lobster lunch.

Restaurant lobsters are officially classified and priced as heavyweight, welterweight or featherweight. Top prices are paid for novelty breeds, such as the so-called Pavarotti lobster, which is covered in hair and sings when taken out of the water. This musical, furry lobster was first found by French researchers but they didn't realise it's importance, so they ate it.

Lobsters were never popular in Japan until the mid-1960s, when they introduced 'Catch Your Own Live Lobster' vending machines. The diner operates a claw to grasp the selected lobster and lift it out, and then at the last minute, drop it back in the tank.

For the purposes of EU classification, lobsters are not considered to be fish, and were previously classified as 'cattle'. The Fisheries Guild objected to this as it made lobsters liable for VAT, whereas crabs are not. They won their case and lobsters, like crabs, are now classified as biscuits.

Oscar Wilde used to take a lobster for walks on a piece of string. When James Abbott McNeill Whistler met him in the street and pointed out that his lobster was dead, Wilde replied, 'Shut your face, Whistler.'

Lobsters are also known as elephant prawns, because of their habit of hanging on to the tail of the animal in front as they march across the sea floor, like elephants round a circus ring. The kangaroo prawn is in fact a small lobster that is able to leap right out of the water to catch passing insects. Just like kangaroos do.

Charles Darwin spent many years searching for two lobsters that he could show were absolutely identical, but sadly he only found one.

Morning TV hunk Adrian Chiles is allergic to lobsters. He's only eaten lobster once, but his face swelled up overnight.

When he was writing his *Petite Larousse Gatronomique*, Alexis Soyer asked several of his fellow chefs how they would define the flavour of lobster. The taste was variously described as 'like a fish masquerading as a mushroom', 'rather like crocodile tail', or 'the flavour of mildewed chicken'. In the book, Soyer compromised and just described the flavour as 'a bit lobstery'.

The low-budget 1964 horror movie *Vengeance of the Lobsterwoman* provided Meryl Streep with her first starring role, opposite Roger Moore who played the Lobsterwoman.

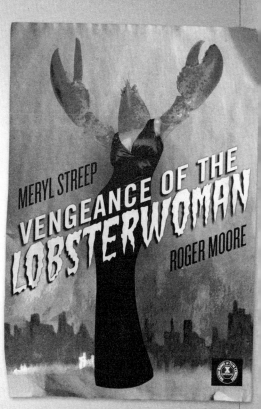

FACT ⊕ : The musical, furry lobster was first found by French researchers but they didn't realise it's importance, so they ate it.

FACT ⊕ : In Japan they introduced 'Catch Your Own Live Lobster' vending machines.

FACT ⊕ : Oscar Wilde used to take a lobster for walks on a piece of string.

FACT ⊕ : Lobsters are also known as elephant prawns, because of their habit of hanging on to the tail of the animal in front as they march across the sea floor.

FACT ⊕ : The flavour of lobster was variously described as 'rather like crocodile tail'.

LONDON UNDERGROUND

INTERIOR OF CARRIAGE.

Tube carriages originally had buttoned upholstery and no windows and were nicknamed 'padded cells'.

The first underground electric railway, the City and South London, which ran from near the Bank of England under the Thames to the South Bank, opened in 1890. It was the first line to be called 'the Tube'.

When the first escalator was installed on the London Underground, to reassure people that it was safe, a man with a wooden leg called 'Bumper' Harris was hired to travel up and down it continuously for a week.

This first escalator was installed at Earl's Court in 1911, and the one-legged 'Bumper' Harris was employed to demonstrate its safety. The London Transport Museum's Depot in Acton boasts a tiny model 'Bumper' Harris in celebration of the man's important role in the history of the escalator.

Harry Beck, designer of the Tube map, was paid only five guineas (£5.25) for the copyright to his work by London Underground.

Harry Beck produced the well-known Tube map diagram in 1931, having been made redundant from his job as an engineering draughtsman at the London Underground Signals Office. The map was

rejected at first, but after a successful small print run of 500 copies, it was accepted in 1932. In 1933, 700,000 copies were printed, and a further print run was required within a month. Beck continued to revise his original design as new stations were added until 1960, when a dispute over his map's remodelling by other designers led to a rift with his former employers. Beck died in 1974 – still bitter about how the map had been taken from his control. Today Beck's map has generated considerably more money for London Underground than its trains ever have.

For many years the recording of 'Mind The Gap' on the Piccadilly Line was spoken by David Archer from Radio 4's *The Archers.*

David Archer is played by the actor Tim Bentinck, or to give him his full title, Timothy Charles Robert Noel Bentinck, 12th Earl of Portland, Viscount Woodstock and Baron Cirencester.

Travelling on the Tube for 40 minutes is the equivalent of smoking two cigarettes.

According to research by University College, London, such is the concentration of dust particles, that travelling on the Underground for 40 minutes is the equivalent to smoking two cigarettes.

LORD BYRON

Lord Byron duped female admirers requesting a lock of his hair by sending them instead hair belonging to his pet dog.

The handsome dog was a Newfoundland called Boatswain.

Byron had four pet geese that travelled in cages under his carriage, and accompanied him to social gatherings.

His friend, the poet Shelley, writes that Byron kept a retinue of animals: 'ten horses, eight enormous dogs, three monkeys, five cats, an eagle, a crow and a falcon; and all these except the horses, walk about the house, which every now and then resounds with their unarbitrated quarrels, as if they were masters of it'. In addition Byron kept a pet fox, heron, badger and crocodile.

Lord Byron served wine to his visitors in a human skull.

Byron found the skull in the cloisters of his home, Newstead Abbey, and wrote of its discovery: 'The gardener in digging discovered a skull that had probably belonged to some jolly friar or monk of the abbey about the time it was dismonasteried. Observing it to be of giant size and in a perfect state of preservation, a strange fancy seized me of having it set and mounted as a drinking cup.'

Lord Byron was anorexic.

Byron's anorexia nervosa was diagnosed by his doctors as brain disease, and would, according to 19th century medical opinion, be the inevitable result of his life of sin. He was also noted to suffer from biliousness, chilblains and convulsions. Contrary to his popular image, Byron was born with red hair and a club foot for which he was obliged to wear a special boot and brace throughout his life.

When Lord Byron's body was exhumed in 1938, one spectator noted the 'quite abnormal development' exhibited, even in death, by the poet's phallus.

In the summer of 1938, a small group assembled in the parish church at Hucknall Torkard to investigate the condition of Lord Byron in his coffin in the family vault. When the coffin lid was raised, Byron's body – minus his lungs and larynx, which had been briefly enshrined in western Greece – was revealed to be in an excellent state of preservation.

LUDWIG VAN BEETHOVEN

The composer Haydn, who taught Beethoven, failed to recognise his student's talent and advised Beethoven to give up writing music.

When Beethoven took his Piano Concerto No. 1 to Joseph Haydn, who had taught him harmony as a student, Haydn's only comment was: 'It is very average. Just play music and don't bother writing music.' In a separate incident, Haydn recommended Beethoven attempt to gain musical credibility by referring to himself as 'Pupil of Haydn'.

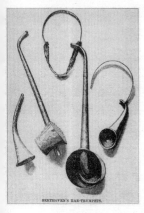

BEETHOVEN'S EAR-TRUMPETS.

To compensate for his deafness, Beethoven would 'hear' the music by placing a stick on the top of his piano and biting on it.

Beethoven suffered from a form of sclerosis which causes the three bones in the inner ear to shrink, and is curable today with a minor operation. It did mean however that he could hear the piano by putting a wooden stick between it and his head, thereby using vibrations to the skull to transmit the sound to the inner ear.

Beethoven was once arrested after being mistaken for a tramp.

Beethoven was inclined to dress in a very scruffy manner and was reported to the local constable in Baden after being seen peering in at people's windows one evening. When the constable arrested him for vagrancy, he protested: 'But I am Beethoven.' 'You're a tramp,' was the reply, and Beethoven was locked up till the following morning.

Coffee lover Beethoven insisted that every cup of coffee made for him was prepared from exactly 60 coffee beans.

According to Anton Schindler, an associate and biographer of Beethoven: 'For breakfast he drank coffee which he usually prepared in a glass coffee maker. He estimated sixty beans to the cup and would often count them out.'

The opening bars of Beethoven's Fifth Symphony preceded all BBC radio broadcasts to Europe during the Second World War because it sounded like the Morse code for the letter 'V' for victory.

The opening consists of three quick Gs and a long E-flat, similar to the three dots and one dash of Morse code. This symbolism resonated into Belgium, where the 'V' also came to represent 'Victoire', and the Netherlands, where the 'V' meant 'Vreiheidt,' or freedom. People also enjoyed the irony of using German music to speak for the Allied efforts to defeat the Nazis.

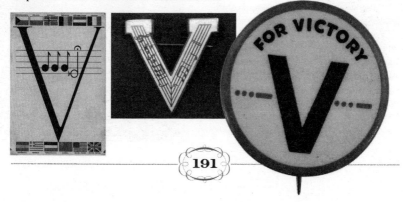

MARRIAGE

50 per cent of marriages in Pakistan are between first cousins.

And in the UK, 55 per cent of marriages among Pakistanis are between first cousins. Marrying within the extended families allows Pakistanis to maintain the concept of birandari, or 'brotherhood' differences. Marriages between first and second cousins account for over 10 per cent of marriages worldwide, and Professor Robin Fox believes that it is likely that 80 per cent of all marriages in history have been between second cousins or closer relatives.

Wedding cake was originally thrown at the bride and groom, not eaten by them.

In medieval times, the cake was made of wheat and thrown at the bride as a symbol of fertility. Additionally, all the baked goods that were to be eaten after the ceremony were piled into a high mound, over which the couple would attempt to kiss. If they managed this feat without sending the pile tumbling, superstition said they would have a lifetime of prosperity.

Wedding rings are worn on the fourth finger of the left hand because the Romans believed a nerve led directly from there to the heart.

The Latin name for the vein was 'Vena Amoris', or vein of love, although we now know that all the fingers have similar vein structures.

In Utah, first-cousin marriages are legal as long as you are 65 or older.

Although Utah law states that you can't marry a first cousin or closer relative, it will allow marriages between the over 65s, or where both parties are 55 or over and the court finds they are unable to reproduce.

States Allowing Marriage Between First Cousins

Bachelors are three times more likely to go mad than married men.

In 1927, Professor G.M. Robertson, President of the Edinburgh Royal College of Physicians, reported that: 'Young men between 25 and 35 years of age continuing bachelors died, on the average, four years sooner than married men, and ran three times the risk of becoming insane. The incidence of insanity among the married was decidedly low, but it was increased in a marked degree by the loss of a husband or wife.'

MICE

Baby Mouse Wine is a bottle of wine packed with baby mice, to add flavour.

A popular 'health tonic' in China and Korea, the wine is made by adding a large number of 2-3 day old baby mice to a bottle of rice wine and leaving to ferment for 12 months. The wine is believed to cure colds and liver problems.

When mice are in the mood for love, they burst into song.

Mice whistle and sing like birds, but at a pitch too high for human ears to hear. Scientists believe these songs are linked to happiness. The male mouse sings a complex chirping song throughout sex, but the female mouse is more likely to sing during social reunion with other females, and only squeaks uncomfortably during sex.

The east Australian brown 'antechinus' mouse can spend up to 12 hours mating with different partners.

To do this, the males strip their body of vital proteins and also suppress the immune system to free up additional metabolic energy. As a result, the exhausted males die after the breeding season.

In the Arctic, mice-cream is a speciality dish.

Arctic explorers call it '*souris à la crème*', with Canadian conservationist Farley Mowat

advising that the best results are achieved by sautéing the mice without removing their heads.
1. Skin, gut and wash some fat mice without removing their heads.
2. Cover them in a pot with ethyl alcohol and marinate two hours.
   Cut a piece of salt pork or sowbelly into small dice and cook it slowly to extract the fat.
3. Drain the mice, dredge them thoroughly in a mixture of flour, pepper and salt, and fry slowly in the rendered fat for about five minutes.
4. Add a cup of alcohol and six to eight cloves, cover and simmer for 15 minutes.
5. Prepare a cream sauce, transfer the sautéed mice to it, and warm them in it for about 10 minutes before serving.

In the 18th century, it was considered the height of fashion to wear false eyebrows made out of mouse skin.

The fashion was a result of French wigs that started so far back on the head, women needed to shave their real eyebrows and glue the mouse skin falsies further up their foreheads in order to keep the wide eyed and innocent look prized at the time. This poem was written by Matthew Prior in 1718:

> *On little things, as sages write*
> *Depends our human joy or sorrow;*
> *If we don't catch a mouse to-night,*
> *Alas! no eyebrows for to-morrow*

MILK

The Queen's milk is delivered in special bottles with her monogram on them.

The Queen has her own lavish dairy, based at Windsor's royal farm, which has fountains at either end of the milking parlour. The 10 cows provide milk for the royal kitchens, and the first time Elizabeth II reportedly realised she was actually Queen was when she saw milk bottles with 'E II R' on them. As a child, the Queen wanted to marry a farmer and 'have lots of cows' when she grew up.

If you burst a paper bag near the ear of a Jersey cow, its milk flow will be interrupted for about 30 minutes.

This was shown in an experiment conducted in Kentucky in 1941, which also found that after 30 minutes, only 70 per cent of normal milk production resumed. Injections of adrenalin had a similar effect, so the stoppage in production is believed to be caused by the adrenalin released by fright.

People in Siberia buy their milk frozen.

In winter-time in Siberia, which lasts from October till May, the milk is sold in chunks instead of pints. It has sometimes been frozen onto a stick to provide a handy carrying handle.

The greatest distance walked by a person continuously balancing a milk bottle on the head is 80.96 miles.

The record holder is Ashrita Furman of New York, and it took him 23 hours 35 minutes to complete the walk. Furman is a Guinness World Records record-breaker, and has the official record for 'the most current Guinness World Records held at the same time by an individual'. He has set more than 400 Guinness Records since 1979 and currently holds 151 Guinness records.

The earliest reference to 'skimmed milk' is by Shakespeare in _Henry IV, Part I_.

In the folio edition of _Henry IV, Part I_, from 1623, it reads: 'Oh, I could divide myself and go to buffets, for moving such a dish of skim'd milk with so honourable an action.'

MONEY

Until the 19th century, compressed blocks of tea were used as money in Siberia.

Due to the high value of tea in many parts of Asia, 'tea bricks' were used as a form of currency in China and parts of Central Asia, and because they could be eaten as food in times of hunger, tea bricks were preferred over metallic coins by the nomads of Siberia and Mongolia. Tea bricks were being made in Russia as late as 1891.

Our word 'salary' is derived from the Roman tradition of paying legionnaires' monthly salaries in salt.

This was known as 'salt money' or 'salarium', and is also the origin of the phrase 'worth their salt'. The Roman Republic closely controlled the price of salt, increasing it to pay for wars, or lowering it to ensure poor citizens could afford it.

During the French Revolution playing cards were used as currency, with the 'court cards' appearing as higher denominations.

This 'improvised currency' became popular when denominations of the new French government's paper money proved too high for the needs of most people. And the first paper money to appear in North America was also printed on playing cards. In 1686 the French colony of Canada ran short of francs, and so playing cards were pressed into service in place of bank notes. The practice proved so popular that it continued for the best part of a hundred years.

In America, ransom money paid to a kidnapper is tax deductible.

Ransom money falls into the category of 'theft, blackmail and extortion', but to claim you will need a proof of payment, such as a receipt for the ransom.

The Aztecs used cocoa beans as a form of currency.

According to Hernando de Oviedo y Valdez, who visited America in 1513, 100 cocoa beans could buy you a slave, 4 cocoa beans, a rabbit and 10 cocoa beans the services of a prostitute.

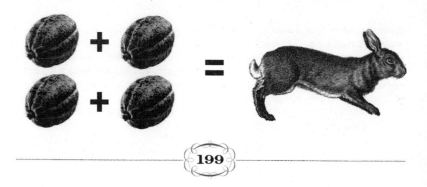

MONKEYS

In the First World War, a monkey was promoted to the rank of corporal.

Corporal Jackie of the 3rd South African infantry was a friendly and highly intelligent baboon, taken to war by South African farmer Albert Marr. A favourite amongst the troops, Jackie was made regimental mascot, issued with rations, uniform and paybook, and described as an 'excellent soldier, always smartly turned out, friendly and respectful, giving a proper salute to every passing officer'. He was injured by a shell in Belgium in 1918, resulting in the amputation of his right leg and a medal for bravery, and returned to live on Marr's farm after the armistice.

In Roman times, one method of execution involved being sewn into a sack with a live dog, cockerel, snake and monkey.

As a punishment for parricide (the killing of a close relative), the convicted person would be blindfolded as unworthy of light, stripped, whipped with rods, sewn with the animals into a sack known as a culeus, and thrown into the sea.

Rhesus macaques will 'pay' to look at pictures of the faces and bottoms of female monkeys.

An experiment at Duke University, named 'Monkey Pay-Per-View', showed that the monkeys will pay to look at pictures of high-ranking females by forfeiting their usual reward of a glass of cherry juice, but have to be bribed with a larger than usual glass of juice to pay attention to photos of low-ranking females. Neurobiologist Dr Michael Platt believes this may help explain our fascination with celebrities.

Deep-fried monkey toes are eaten in Indonesia.

They are served like chicken wings, and eaten by sucking the meat straight off the bone. The Indonesians also eat smoked bats.

The first spelling of what we now call a monkey wrench or spanner was 'monckeh' after its inventor Charles Moncke.

Mr Moncke was a 17th century London blacksmith, presumably of German extraction, whose foreign-sounding name is likely to have been pronounced 'monkey' by locals.

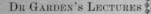
MRS BEETON

Mrs Beeton was allergic to pork and had, in some people's eyes, an irrational dislike of carrots. Her love and obsession with 'the other root', the parsnip, was legendary, and she even gave her name to the dark red variety of turnip – the beetroot.

In her cookbook, *Simple Cooking for Common Folk*, she doesn't include eggs in any one of the 2,036 recipes. She devotes a whole chapter to whipping cream which she says is best done wearing a tight rubber corset. This racy material greatly upset her husband Randolph Beeton, who wouldn't allow roast chicken to be served at his table unless it was wearing trousers.

She believed in healthy eating, and thanks to her policy of five a year for fruit and veg, plus a daily intake of lard, Mrs Beeton herself lived to the ripe old age of 29.

It's little wonder Mrs Beeton became so handy in the kitchen as she was one of 34 children. Thanks to being born with a dodgy knee she was not involved in the family football team, consigned instead to knocking out half-time oranges and full-time sandwiches.

In fact she only took up cooking in the last three months of her life. Her attempts at a career had previously been marked by failure. Her first job as a stunt double for Charlotte

Brontë had to be abandoned when her bad knee let her down during a saloon brawl. She failed to make a success as a circus clown, and her career as the Paris racing correspondent for *Sporting Life* was ended when she tried to burn down a cheese factory in Montmartre. When asked what she had against cheese, Mrs Beeton stated famously that 'decomposing corpses are not wholesome eating'.

As a matter of fact, in later editions of her book, her chapter on cannibalism is omitted, following complaints from readers who found her recipes disappointingly bland.

When she died, Mrs Beeton's body lay undiscovered for three days, before her husband

finally lost patience and burst into the kitchen shouting, 'how long do we have to wait for this bloody casserole?' Upon realising the gruesome truth, Mr Beeton kept his wife's death a secret from the public, fearing that the news would have an adverse affect on the sales of her book. The casserole, however, was delicious.

The casserole was actually from a recipe book by Eliza Acton, from whom Mrs Beeton shamelessly stole many ideas including her recipe for Pot Noodles.

Christmas Plum Pudding.

FACT ❺ : The casserole was actually from a recipe book by Eliza Acton, from whom Mrs Beeton shamelessly stole many ideas.

FACT ❹ : Mr Beeton kept his wife's death a secret from the public, fearing that the news would have an adverse affect on the sales of her book.

FACT ❸ : Mrs Beeton stated famously that 'decomposing corpses are not wholesome eating'.

FACT ❷ : She was the Paris racing correspondent for *Sporting Life*.

FACT ❶ : Mrs Beeton herself lived to the ripe old age of 29.

MUSHROOMS

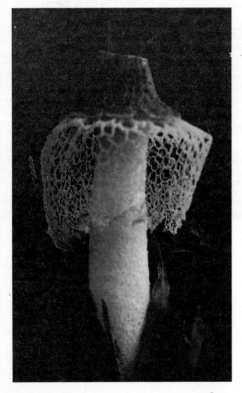

The Veiled Lady mushroom takes just 20 minutes to attain its full height of eight inches, its cells expanding at such a rate that they make an audible cracking sound.

Mushrooms often grow fast as they increase in size through cell enlargement, which requires very little energy.

Portobello mushrooms are the result of a marketing ploy: before the 1980s, Portobello mushrooms were just called brown mushrooms, which growers usually had to throw away as they couldn't sell them.

Portobello mushrooms are overgrown brown button or crimini mushrooms, whose size leads to an opening of the mushroom's gills, which in turn causes the mushroom to dry out and to acquire its now prized meaty texture.

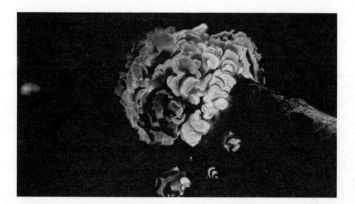

Mushrooms were used to provide lighting in the first submarines to be used in battle.

Foxfire mushrooms were used in a submarine called 'The Turtle', which was first used in 1776 against the British during the American War of Independence. Benjamin Franklin suggested the use of foxfire mushrooms as lighting due to the mushrooms' bioluminescence – they grow green in the dark when combined with decaying wood.

The largest living thing in the world is a mushroom with a diameter of three and a half miles.

Officially known as 'Armillaria ostoyae', the honey mushroom is located in the Malheur National Forest in eastern Oregon, where it covers approximately 2,200 acres.

Mushroom soup is frequently used in the film industry to replicate vomit.

Actress Drew Barrymore mixed together cream of mushroom soup and stuffing to make her vomit look authentic on the set of comedy *Our House*, although Linda Blair preferred to use pea soup in *The Exorcist*.

NOSES

The captain of the *Beagle* nearly rejected Charles Darwin as the ship's naturalist due to the shape of his nose.

The temperamental captain Robert Fitzroy studied physiognomy and the work of Lavater, and believed he could judge a man's character by the outline of his features. He thought Darwin's nose was too broad and squat for him to possess the necessary energy and determination to survive the difficult journey.

The buttons on a man's jacket cuff were originally intended to stop menservants wiping their noses on the sleeves of their uniforms.

And in the Victorian era, mourning clothes too were specifically designed with buttons on the cuff to stop men wiping their noses on them when crying. Women however wore buttonless nine-inch white cuffs referred to as 'weepers', as they could use them to wipe the nose during crying fits.

A man from China can pull a car with his nose, as well as using his nose to inflate the inner tube of a truck tyre in only ten minutes.

Zhang Zhenghui, of Liling, even managed to fend off competition from two young men inflating an identical tyre with bicycle pumps. Zhang's 'Nose Pulling Car' stunt involves attaching one side of a rope to a car and the other to his nose via a harness.

18th century Yorkshireman Thomas Wedders had a nose that measured seven and a half inches long.

Wedders put his nose to good use by joining a travelling show, and exhibited his pronounced proboscis throughout Yorkshire in the 1770s. In his *Anomalies and Curiosities of Medicine* George Milbry Gould wrote: 'This man expired as he had lived, in a condition of mind best described as the most abject idiocy.'

In 1837, Thomas Saverland had part of his nose bitten off by a woman after he tried to kiss her.

Saverland took the woman, Miss Caroline Newton, to court, but lost, the judge commenting, 'When a man kisses a woman against her will, she is fully entitled to bite his nose, if she so pleases.'

NUDITY

In Britain, the law forbids boys under 10 from looking at naked mannequins.

This archaic law dates from the reign of George V in the early 20th century, when mannequins first began to appear in shop windows. The obligation is to the shopkeeper to keep the mannequins covered rather than for those boys under 10 to avert their gaze.

Internet auction site eBay was hit by a craze in which sellers appear naked in reflections on goods they're selling.

The exhibitionist craze came to be known as 'reflectoporn'.

The first actress to appear naked in a moving picture in 1896 was called Louise Willy.

Within a year of the first public showing of a moving picture, Willy appeared naked in a 7-minute silent French film called *Le Coucher de la Mariée* (Bedtime for the Bride). Willy performed a striptease during a bath scene.

Ancient Chinese artists freely painted scenes of nudity and sex, but they would never depict a naked female foot.

The Chinese used to bind women's feet so they didn't look like feet anymore. Pointing the soles of the feet at someone in Thailand is the height of bad manners. The Japanese on the other hand wouldn't depict the nape of a woman's neck, as they thought that was the sexiest bit.

In March 2004 a boat on Lake Travis in Texas capsized after all the passengers rushed to one side as the boat passed Texas's only nudist beach.

The accident occurred at the Hippie Hollow clothing-optional area during Splash Day, a semi-annual event hosted by the Austin Tavern Guild, a gay and lesbian bar association. The party boat was filled with 60 men and women at the time, and two people were hospitalised.

NUTS

To protect their winter food stocks from potential thieves, grey squirrels put on an elaborate show of burying non-existent nuts and seeds.

They even go so far as to cover them over with soil to dupe any thieving onlookers. It's estimated that millions of trees in the world are accidentally planted by grey squirrels that bury nuts and then forget where they've hidden them.

Brazil nuts are radioactive.

While all foods contain small amounts of natural radioactivity, the Brazil nut contains more radium-226 than any other food – up to 7,000 times more.

Pistachios are classified under the International Maritime Dangerous Goods code.

Fresh pistachios, if stacked under pressure, can burst into flames and cause a cargo fire. They are especially

dangerous when stowed with fibrous material, as the oil-soaked fabrics promote combustion. Peanuts have been used in the manufacture of dynamite, as peanut oil can be processed to produce glycerol, which can be used to make nitro-glycerine, one of the constituents of dynamite.

If you shake a can of mixed nuts, the larger nuts will rise to the top.

This is called 'granular convection', or the 'Brazil nut effect', and is caused by vertical vibrations acting with the rough, vertical walls.

The Ancient Greeks believed that walnuts could cure head ailments, since they're shaped like a brain.

Greek physician Dioscorides promoted a version of the 'doctrine of signatures', believing that plants resembling organs and body parts could be used as effective cures for those same body parts. He also thought walnuts had a variety of medicinal uses, and advocated that they were eaten with rue and figs to counteract poisons, with honey and rue to 'ease inflammation of the breasts, abscesses and dislocations', and with onions, salt and honey to heal dog bites.

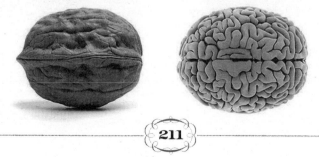

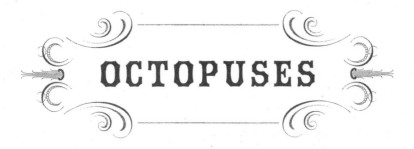

OCTOPUSES

An octopus can undo the lid of a screw-top jar.

They do this by pressing their body onto the lid and grasping the sides with their eight tentacles. There are many examples of octopuses learning to do this in order to reach food in the jar, and some have even managed to open childproof lids on medicine bottles.

Octopuses have been observed to eat their own arms.

It was once believed the octopus did this due to stress, but it's now thought to be the result of a neurological disorder prompted by a virus which attacks the octopus's nervous system towards the end of its life.

The correct plural of octopus is 'octopodes'.

The word 'octopi' has no etymological basis, as octopus comes from Ancient Greek rather than Latin, where its plural is 'ocopodes'. Octopuses is the most commonly used plural form, including in scientific writing.

The female blanket octopus is 40,000 times heavier than the male.

The diminutive male, who is also 100 times smaller, mates with the female by filling a modified tentacle with sperm, tearing it off and presenting it to their prospective mate, who will then hide it in an internal body cavity until it is time for her to tear it open and pour the sperm over her eggs.

Some octopuses use coconut shells as armour and wield snapped-off jellyfish tentacles as weapons.

The blanket octopus is immune to the man o' war sting, so it will rip off its stinging tentacles and carry them around, using them as a weapon. The veined octopus carries coconut shell halves as portable armour to hide behind in case it's threatened.

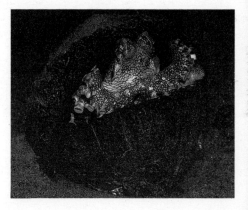

THE OLYMPICS

The Olympic flame has been carried by more famous novelists than any other well-known flame. For the 1964 Games it was carried by Jeffrey Archer on the tricky Dover to Calais leg. Holding the precious flame aloft he completed the cross Channel swim in a time of 2 hours and 13 minutes, beating the previous record held by the P&O ferry.

The distance of the marathon is the rather strange figure of 26 miles and 385 yards because at the 1908 London Games, Queen Alexandra demanded that after completing the 26 miles, the runners should carry on another 385 yards to the finishing line right in front of the royal box.

One early field event was catching the shot – a ball fired from a small cannon. In 1912, after several athletes had been injured a memo was sent to the committee: 'Would athletes not be safer throwing the shot rather than trying to catch it? Discuss.' As a result, in the next games, they introduced the shot-putt and accidentally the discus.

Today, some glues are banned in table-tennis bats because as the bats warm up during play they release performance-enhancing fumes (because they make the ball travel 20 mph faster).

Sex-tests for athletes were introduced originally as a competitive event, but abandoned when a satisfactory scoring system couldn't be devised.

At the 1976 Games all female athletes were sex-tested, except for Princess Anne.

Johnny Weissmuller, later to find fame in the movies as King Kong, took part in the 1932 Olympics, and was hotly tipped to win gold in the pool events, but in the semi-finals sadly broke his cue trying for a tricky eight ball.

At the gymnastics in 1976 spectators were outraged when Nadia Comăneci's perfect display was rewarded with a score of only 1. This was because the scoreboards could only display scores up to 9.99 so her perfect 10 was displayed as 1.00.

It is not generally known that Olympic gold medals are actually made of wood, silver medals are made from recycled fish products, and bronze medals are actually gold with a coating of Hammerite paint.

A popular trivia question is 'In which year did nobody win the pentathlon?'. The answer is 1956, the year when Finland's Pavo Nobdy won the event.

The most famous dead heat came in the 1948 Games when both Yrjö Lindegren of Finland and Adolph Hoch of Austria took the gold medal for Architecture both having designed identical buildings.

FACT ❶ : In the 1948 Games Adolph Hoch of Austria took the gold medal for Architecture.

FACT ❷ : At the gymnastics in 1976 spectators were outraged when Nadia Comăneci's perfect display was rewarded with a score of only 1. This was because the scoreboards could only display scores up to 9.99 so her perfect 10 was displayed as 1.00.

FACT ❸ : At the 1976 Games all female athletes were sex-tested, except for Princess Anne.

FACT ❹ : Today, some glues are banned in table-tennis bats.

FACT ❺ : The distance of the marathon is the rather strange figure of 26 miles and 385 yards because at the 1908 London Games, Queen Alexandra demanded that after completing the 26 miles, the runners should carry on another 385 yards to the finishing line right in front of the royal box.

215

ORANGE

When an orange is shown in any of the *Godfather* movies, it means a character is about to die or have a close call.

For example: Don Corleone buys oranges right before he is shot; Sonny drives past an advertisement for Florida oranges before he is assassinated; at the Mafioso summit, bowls of oranges are placed in front of those Dons who will be assassinated; before Don Corleone dies, he puts an orange peel in his mouth to playfully scare his grandson; and Tessio, who is executed for attempting to betray Michael, plays with an orange at Connie's wedding.

If you feed yellow canaries with red peppers, they turn orange.

This trick was common practice amongst English canary breeders in the 1870s, and succeeds because peppers are high in carotenoid pigments. Other foods that can have this effect include sweet potatoes, tomatoes, paprika and cherries, and it is possible to turn canaries a deep red if you feed them a concentrate carotenoids mix, although this can result in liver and kidney damage. Similarly, many flamingos in captivity are fed pink dyes to prevent them turning white when removed from their natural diet of carotenoid rich algae and crustaceans.

Blorenge and Gorringe are the only two rhymes for orange in English, and both are proper nouns.

Gorringe is the 6,313th most popular surname in the UK, and Blorenge is a hill overlooking the Usk river valley in Southeast Wales. However, depending on pronunciation, some people have argued that they are merely half rhymes, grouping them with words such as hinge, lozenge, syringe and flange.

Beavers have bright orange teeth.

The enamel on the front of the tooth contains orange-coloured iron for extra strength, meaning that the softer backside of the tooth wears faster as they chew wood. Because beaver teeth also grow continuously, this creates self-sharpening teeth.

In California it is illegal to peel an orange in your hotel room.

In California, it is also illegal to trip horses for entertainment; a man is legally entitled to beat his wife with a leather belt or strap, but the belt cannot be wider than two inches, unless he has his wife's consent to beat her with a wider strap; and the city of Mountain View forbids calling pet fish by 'names of aggressive content, such as "biter", "killer" or "sugar-ray".'

OSCAR WILDE

Oscar Wilde's mother dressed him as a girl for the first few years of his life.

Clothing for Victorian children was not particularly gender specific, and it was common for infant boys to wear dresses – it assisted in the process of nappy changing. However, it is believed that Lady Jane Wilde went further than was normal, including covering young Oscar with jewels, as she had hoped for a girl.

Oscar Wilde took a dead lobster for walks on a piece of string.

While studying at Oxford University, Oscar would walk through the streets with a lobster on a leash. This may have been an homage to the French romantic poet Gérard de Nerval who had a pet lobster named Thibault which he took for walks in the Palais Royal gardens on the end of a blue silk ribbon.

Oscar Wilde was editor of *The Woman's World* magazine.

This job took up two mornings a week, for which he was paid a weekly salary of £6. He changed the title from the original *The Lady's World*, and managed to entice contributions from distinguished figures such as the Queen of Romania, Princess Christian and actress Sarah Bernhard, who wrote an essay entitled 'The History Of My Tea Gown'. Wilde approached Queen Victoria to submit poems, but she declined.

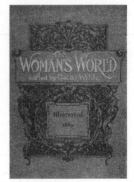

In 2004, a London musical about Oscar Wilde closed after only one night.

Written by former Radio 1 DJ Mike Read, the show was described as invoking feelings of 'incredulous contempt' by the *Daily Telegraph,* and the *Guardian* wondered whether 'the sound system was being affected by the hefty rumbling of Oscar Wilde turning in his grave'.

An angel figure on Oscar Wilde's grave in Père Lachaise cemetery had its penis snapped off in an act of vandalism.

It was reported that the statue's penis, designed by Jacob Epstein, was then used as a paperweight by the cemetery superintendent. In 2000, an artist held a ceremony where a silver prosthetic was attached in its place. Wilde has two graves, both with headstones. The other is at Bagneux cemetery.

OSTRICHES

No ostrich has ever been observed to bury its head in the sand.

Contrary to popular belief, this is not natural ostrich behaviour, and in fact an ostrich would suffocate if it did so. It is thought that this myth originated from Roman historian Pliny the Elder, who observed ostriches asleep with their necks stretched forward on the ground, or with faces close to the ground when swallowing small pebbles to aid digestion. In reality, ostriches simply run away when faced with danger, something they do well, being the fastest animal in the world on two legs (ostriches have been clocked at speeds of over 40 miles an hour, which they can maintain for at least 30 minutes, making them faster than a racehorse).

For hundreds of years it was believed that ostriches hatched their eggs by looking at them.

The idea that ostriches could hatch their eggs by looking at them aggressively was another ostrich misconception spread by Pliny the Elder. The belief still prevailed in medieval Europe, with several Christian texts asserting that the ostrich incubates its eggs by staring at them.

A male ostrich can roar like a lion.

The ostrich has a booming warning call that sounds like a lion's roar. This is the basis for an African folk tale, where the lioness is impressed with the ostrich, and declares him her match.

The Ancient Egyptians trained ostriches to pull carts.

More than 2,000 years ago, an Egyptian queen, Arsinoe, even rode an ostrich with a saddle. Some South African ranchers have trained ostriches to act as shepherds for their flocks of sheep. In the United States, a tourist attraction in South Pasadena called 'Cawston Ostrich Farm' opened in 1886, becoming America's first ostrich farm and one of California's most famous early attractions. Visitors could ride on the backs of ostriches or be taken for ostrich-drawn carriage rides, as well as buying ostrich-feathered hats, boas, capes and fans at the farm shop.

Ostriches yawn in groups before going to sleep.

There have been entire scientific studies devoted to this topic, including 'Yawning and Other Maintenance Activities in the South African Ostrich' by E.G. Franz Sauer and E.M. Sauer.

PAINTING

The Scottish biologist Alexander Fleming used multi-coloured bacteria to create germ paintings.
The bacteria were invisible when he painted them on, but became colourful as they grew. Fleming created a variety of images from simple faces and stick characters to more detailed creations such as the house cavalryman pictured above. Fleming was a keen amateur watercolour painter and member of the Chelsea Arts Club.

As a young man, Picasso was so poor that he kept warm by burning his own pictures.
Having parted ways with his financial backers, and yet to find commercial success, Picasso's financial situation in 1902 was so dire he couldn't afford winter fuel.

Legend has it that Greek painter Zeuxis laughed himself to death at the sight of one of his own paintings.

Zeuxis was painting a vain old lady at the time, and supposedly laughed so hard he fatally broke a blood vessel. Rembrandt once completed a self-portrait of himself as the cackling Greek.

A pair of Croatian dog-lovers painted their house white with black spots in memory of their dead pet Dalmatian.

Goran and Karmen Tomasich were so upset when their pet Bingo was run over by a car, they painted their house in his memory. The couple say they were worried about what the neighbours would think, but were determined to let everyone know how much they loved Bingo.

Rapper Kanye West has a version of the Sistine Chapel ceiling painted in his dining room.

Influenced by the famous roof, West paid artist Ernie Barnes to decorate his ceiling with a piece called 'A Life Restored', depicting the rapper being saved by an angel after he nearly died in a car accident. He has said that the Sistine Chapel also influenced the set of his 2010 music video *Power*, which he described as a 'moving painting'.

PANDAS

Vets in China have shown 'panda porn' to captive pandas in an attempt to encourage them to mate.

Conservationists have been trying to breed pandas in captivity for many years but it has proved extremely difficult as female giant pandas are fertile for just three days a year and seem to lose their sexual appetite once in captivity. Giving the males Viagra and showing panda couples 'panda pornography' – film of mating pairs – had limited success. Artificial insemination has proved the most successful way of boosting the captive panda population.

Pandas are carnivores.

They have carnivore teeth, designed for ripping and chewing meat, and have been known to eat other animals. This might explain why their digestive system is so inefficient at processing bamboo.

Giant pandas bleat like sheep.

Adult pandas make a variety of noises, including roars, growls and honks, and young panda cubs are also able to make a croaking noise. The bleat is thought to be important in selecting a mate during the brief two- or three-day window each year when the female is fertile. Males with longer bleats have been found to have higher levels of testosterone, and females can differentiate between males based on their bleats.

In 1961, push-button 'panda' crossings were introduced in the UK.

The 45 trial 'panda' road crossings were set up in Guildford, Lincoln and London. Hailed as 'a new idea in pedestrian safety', these consisted of triangular white road markings, belisha beacons with black stripes on top and a series of flashing amber and red lights. Despite a large promotional campaign, the new crossings were met with confusion by road users, and failed to catch on.

It was not until 1985 that DNA analysis finally confirmed that the giant panda is a bear.

Stephen O'Brien published his findings in the science journal *Nature*, finally establishing that pandas are bears and not racoons. The research also confirmed that the lesser, or red, panda is a raccoon, although the giant panda is more closely related to the lesser panda than it is to other bears, due to convergent evolution.

PANTS

In the early 19th century the words 'pants' and 'trousers' were considered obscene in England.

In an age of prudery, the words were thought to conjure indelicate and erotic images of men's bare legs. Instead, women referred to trousers as 'inexpressibles' or 'a pair of dittoes'.

19th century London merchants sold X-ray-proof underwear.

When the X-ray was discovered by Wilhelm Roentgen in 1895, some journalists were convinced that the primary user of the revealing shortwave radiation would be the 'peeping Tom', and manufacturers of ladies undergarments responded to the concern.

In Japan it's possible to buy used knickers from vending machines in the street.

Such vending machines purportedly sell underpants previously worn by schoolgirls. Despite their being banned in 1993, they are still a regular sight in Japan. Unused underwear is also available via vending machine in Japan.

A US manufacturer has invented underwear with a built-in fart filter.

In 1998, Chester Weimer of Pueblo, Colorado, received a patent for the first airtight undergarment that contained a replaceable charcoal filter. In 2001 Mr Weimer received the Ig Nobel Prize for Biology for his invention, and today there are a number of manufacturers offering 'flatulence filtering underwear'.

In the state of Minnesota, it is against the law to hang male and female underwear together on the same washing-line.

Other strange Minnesotan laws include: it is illegal for a man who has garlic, onions or sardines on his breath to have sex with his wife; and it is against the law for a dog to chase a cat up a telegraph pole, and dog owners can be fined for this.

PENS

When the trade routes to India were first opened up, Indian ink flooded into Europe, so pens had to be invented to use it up. Until then, writing had to be done in pencil. Incidentally, the name 'rubber' was given to the bouncy stuff first harvested from the trees of Indonesia because it could be used to 'rub out' pencil marks.

The earliest recorded use of a pen with a steel nib was when King John signed the Magna Carta. Another first was recorded when William de Clare, Earl of Norfolk, placed the document to be signed in front of the King and said, 'It's not for me it's for my nephew.'

In days gone by, quills for right-handed writers came from the left wing of a goose, while pens for left-handers came from the right. This resulted in flocks of lop-sided geese which could only fly in circles.

The original Parker pen was so popular that, for a time, writing became known as parking. Sheets of paper were known as parking spaces.

Because recording accurate readings of longitude was notoriously difficult, a clockwork pen was developed at the Royal Greenwich Observatory in 1760 for use at sea, but it didn't work. Thomas Edison invented an electric pen which never really caught on except in tattoo parlours, and the nuclear pen, proposed by Enrico Fermi was never developed as it was considered too dangerous.

The ball point pen was first developed by the Rumanian Laszlo Ballpoint. Ballpoint is sometimes confused with the great Hungarian hypnotist Biro, who actually invented the automatic gearbox, which he named after his wife, Gearbox Biro.

Roald Dahl famously wrote all his books with the same pen, which he had designed himself. Dahl's everlasting pen was connected by a tube to a vat of blue ink, fed by a pump powered by small boys chained to a treadmill.

In the state of South Carolina it is against the law to carry more than three pens upon your person, and in Gumpatch, Missouri, it is illegal to know how to write. This law is not as inconvenient as you might think, as in Gumpatch it is also against the law to read.

Inventor Wayne Leigh devised a pen especially for travelling salespersons. To keep their clothes from getting creased overnight, the ballpoint pen converts into a coat-hanger. He went on to invent the wristwatch that converts into a three-piece suit.

At school, Sean Penn's nickname was 'Inky.'

FACT ❶ : The name 'rubber' was given to the bouncy stuff first harvested from the trees of Indonesia because it could be used to rub out, pencil marks.

FACT ❷ : Quills for right-handed writers came from the left wing of a goose, while pens for left-handers came from the right.

FACT ❸ : Thomas Edison invented an electric pen which never really caught on except in tattoo parlours.

FACT ❹ : Hungarian hypnotist Biro invented the automatic gearbox.

FACT ❺ : Inventor Wayne Leigh devised a pen especially for travelling salespersons. To keep their clothes from getting creased overnight, the ballpoint pen converts into a coat-hanger.

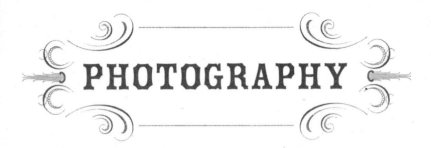

PHOTOGRAPHY

Within 200 yards of the Islington flat where George Orwell had the idea for *1984*, there are now 32 CCTV cameras.

Britain has 4.2 million CCTV cameras, one for every 14 people in the country and 20 per cent of all the CCTV cameras in the world. Croydon has more CCTV cameras than the whole of New York City. It has been calculated that each person in Britain is caught on camera an average of 300 times a day.

The subjects of early photographs had to put their head in a clamp so they could stay still for the long exposures necessary.

The daguerreotype photograph of 1839 required 15- to 30-minute exposures, and so the subject would be placed on a posing chair on a raised platform with their head in a clamp to prevent swaying or movement.

The fastest camera in the world can take up to a trillion photos per second.

The Massachusetts Institute of Technology has developed a camera fast enough to produce a slow-motion video of a burst of light travelling the length of a one-litre bottle, bouncing off the cap and reflecting back again. This is possible because of 'streak camera technology', where light particles are converted into electrons.

In the 1970s, the CIA fixed tiny battery-powered cameras to pigeons and released the birds over enemy targets.

These cameras weighed as little as 20–40 grams, lighter than the camera used in an earlier trial in Washington DC, where the overburdened pigeon was forced to abandon his flight and walk home. The idea of using a pigeon to carry a miniature camera was first patented by a German doctor in 1907.

Forensics students in the 1860s would photograph the eyes of murder victims and look for an image of the perpetrator.

It was a commonly held belief in the latter half of the 19th century that the last image seen by a dying person would be fixed on their retina, and prominent photographers of the time suggested that optograms could be obtained from victims to identify their assailant. The idea was perpetuated by writer Jules Verne and detectives on the Jack the Ripper case were presented with a proposal for using the technique.

Carrier Pigeons Take Aerial Photos With New Camera

IT IS no longer necessary to send planes over enemy lines to get photos of troop operations—carrier pigeons have now been pressed into service for this hazardous task.

This unusual feat is made possible by the development in Germany of a new diminutive aerial camera which is strapped to the pigeon's breast, as illustrated in the accompanying photo. Two hundred views may be taken while in flight, the shots being made possible only after the bird has left the ground. Each bird also carries a message tube strapped to its leg.

The German government has opened a school to train carrier pigeons for service in aerial photography.

PIANOS

The Invalid Piano was a piano specially designed for someone unable to get out of bed.

The piano, with an extending keyboard specially constructed to allow a bed-ridden invalid to play it, was one of the exhibits at the British Industries Fair which opened in White City in 1935.

Princess Alexandra of Bavaria believed that, as a child, she had swallowed a full-sized grand piano made of glass.

The Princess developed this delusion at the age of 23, and thought that the piano remained inside her. It caused her to walk sideways down corridors and through doorways for fear of getting stuck.

Maurice Ravel once wrote a piano piece for a one-handed man.

The famous 'Bolero' composer wrote the piece as a commission for the pianist Paul Wittgenstein, who lost his right arm in the First World War. 'Concerto pour la main gauche en ré majeur' was first performed in Vienna in 1932, and has even featured prominently in an episode of *M*A*S*H*. In contrast, Bach's grandson wrote a concerto for six hands on one piano, to be played by a large man with his arms round two small female pianists.

In Iowa, one-armed piano players must perform for free.

Iowa state law forbids any establishment charging admission to see a one-armed piano player, and also states that a permit is required to place a piano on a sidewalk.

In 1650, Arthanasius Kircher described a 'Cat Piano' played by keys that stuck pins into the tails of cats which mewed at different pitches.

There are no records of the 'Katzenklavier' actually being built, but the design states that the cats should be arranged according to the natural tone of their voices, in order to allow tunes to be played.

Fig. 1. — Un piano de chats. (D'après une gravure du dix-septième siècle.)

PIGEONS

In Europe between the 16th and 18th centuries, pigeon poo was so prized as a fertiliser that armed guards were stationed in front of dovecotes to stop thieves stealing it.

Pigeon guano was considered to be one of the finest fertilisers in the world and was a highly prized commodity as a result. In the Middle East, where eating pigeon flesh was forbidden, dovecotes were built simply to provide manure for growing fruit. The use of armed guards became more common when it was discovered that pigeon guano could also be used to make gunpowder.

The carrier pigeon is the bravest of all animal species; it has received more than half of all the Dickin Medals for Animal Bravery ever issued.

Founded by Mrs Maria Dickin of the People's Dispensary for Sick Animals, thirty-two out of the sixty-two Dickin medals awarded have been to pigeons. Two of the more notable pigeon recipients were Gustav and Paddy, who braved 150 and 230 mile trips to deliver the first accounts of the Normandy Landings. Sadly, Gustav came to a sticky end after the war when someone cleaning out his loft accidentally sat on him.

Pigeons regularly travel from West Ham in East London to Central London on the Tube.

There have also been many other documented cases of pigeons making journeys on the London Underground by boarding at one station and alighting at another. One witness to this behaviour has written: 'From observing the birds, I feel quite sure that travel, not food, was their purpose. Pigeons are intelligent and easily trained and I see no reason why they should not have cottoned on to the fact that travel by Tube saves their wings – especially as there are so many deformed and crippled pigeons in the city.'

In the 1900 Olympics, live pigeons were used as targets in the shooting event.

Live pigeon shooting only appeared once as an Olympic event, and the winner was the participant who shot down the most live birds, after they had been released into the sky. Almost 300 birds were killed in total, turning the event into a bloodbath of feathers and dead and injured birds strewn about the ground. Clay pigeons have been used at all Olympic events since.

In 1970, a performance of the opera *Rigoletto* was brought to an abrupt end when its star swallowed a pigeon feather and fainted.

During the performance in Chile, Canadian baritone Louis Quilico was in the middle of one of his arias when a stray pigeon's feather floated down from the rafters and went straight into his mouth as he threw his head back mid song.

PIGS

A pig's penis is shaped exactly like a corkscrew.

And a female pig has a corkscrew-shaped vagina. The penis is between 45 cm and 62 cm long, and by contracting its retractor muscles, a pig makes its penis move in a semi-rotary fashion.

***The Muppet Show* was banned in Saudi Arabia because one of its stars was a pig.**

Islam regards pigs as unclean animals, and so the presence of Miss Piggy on screen was deemed unacceptable.

In the 19th century, 'learned pigs' amazed audiences with tricks.

The pigs were dressed in waistcoats and travelled throughout Europe performing tricks on command, such as kneeling and bowing, as well as more adventurous tasks like spelling names out and reading minds.

The pig piano, 'Porko Forte' or 'Swineway' was a musical instrument using pigs.

The instrument was commissioned by Louis XI of France in the late 13th century, to provide him with 'a concert of swines' voices'. Built by the Abbot of Beigne, the instrument consisted of pigs of various sizes lined up in a box, which were pricked with little spikes when corresponding keys were played. The King and his company were reportedly delighted with the result.

Some pigs are afraid of mud.

There are reported cases of pigs suffering from 'mysophobia', or a fear of uncleanliness. One such sufferer was a Yorkshire piglet called Cinders, who refused to join her siblings as they splashed around in the mud until her owners kitted her out in tiny wellington boots.

POTATOES

The original Mr Potato Head toy consisted of parts to be stuck into a real potato.

Toy makers Hasbro advertised that you could use 'any fruit or vegetable' to make the funny faces, and also sold a toy car and trailer for your creations to ride around in.

Early cars didn't have windscreen wipers. Instead, drivers rubbed a potato over the glass to help the rainwater run off.

This is due to the wax in the potatoes, and a carrot, onion or chewing tobacco could also be used. The inventor Mary Anderson is credited with devising the first operational windscreen wiper in 1903, some 20 years after the advent of the motor car.

Potatoes were used as currency on the island of Tristan da Cunha until 1942.

In 1946 the first stamps on the island still bore a value in potatoes, to ensure that the inhabitants who didn't use money were able to buy the stamps for four potatoes, rather than four pence.

Until the late 18th century the French believed that potatoes caused leprosy and syphilis.

Although potatoes were a staple food in Ireland by the end of the 17th century, in France they were still believed to cause a variety of fevers well into the 18th century. Between 1773 and 1789, a scientist called Antoine-Augustin Parmentier wrote books and pamphlets urging potato cultivation, and King Louis XVI popularised them by wearing potato flowers in his buttonhole. As late as 1720 in America, eating potatoes was believed to shorten a person's life.

During the famous asteroid scene in *The Empire Strikes Back*, one of the deadly hurtling asteroids is actually a potato.

The potato appears in the top left corner at the beginning of the scene, and there is also a shoe, which was rumoured to have been thrown in by a frustrated special effects crew member, after being asked to reshoot the scene by George Lucas multiple times.

PRINCE PHILIP

Prince Philip was born on a kitchen table.

He was delivered on the kitchen table of his parents' Corfu villa, 'Mon Repos', in 1921. The great-great-grandson of Queen Victoria, and son of Prince Andrew of Greece, Philip was the youngest of five children, and the only boy, yet his inheritance consisted of a few old suits and an ivory-handled shaving brush as his family were exiled and fled the military junta that had overthrown the Greek monarchy.

All four of Prince Philip's sisters married German princes and three became members of the Nazi party.

Sophie, Cecile and Margarita became Nazis, and there are even photographs of the 16-year-old Philip at the 1937 funeral of his elder sister Cecile, flanked by relatives in SS and Brownshirt uniforms. Sophie's husband was a member of the SS and an aide to Heinrich Himmler, and the couple named their first son Karl Adolf in Hitler's honour. However, Philip took pains to distance himself from his German relatives, fighting with distinction for the Allies in the Second World War and changing his name to Lieutenant Philip Mountbatten from the German-sounding family name of Schleswig-Holstein-Sonderburg-Glücksburg. The Prince has explained the attraction of the Nazis at the time in terms of patriotism, economic strength, and the trains running on time.

The cockney rhyming slang for Prince Philip is The Big Bubble.

This derives from the cockney rhyming slang for 'Greek', which is 'Bubble and Squeak'.

The islanders of Tanna worship the Duke of Edinburgh as a god.

Tanna is one of the islands in Vanuatu in the South West Pacific, and the belief is believed to stem from an ancient story about the pale-skinned son of a mountain spirit travelling across the seas to look for a powerful woman to marry. The Prince became associated with this story sometime in the 1960s, possibly as a result of his portrait being present in British colonial police stations, and when he came to visit the area with the Queen in 1974, it was seen as the return of the ancestral spirit, come to show off his bride. The islanders now feast and celebrate on his birthday.

On seeing the President of Nigeria dressed in traditional African robes, Prince Philip told him: 'You look like you're ready for bed.'

This is just one in a long line of culturally insensitive remarks made by the Prince. Others include asking a Scottish driving instructor: 'How do you keep the natives off the booze long enough to pass the test?'; and when visiting China in 1986, Prince Philip told a group of British students: 'If you stay here much longer, you'll all be slitty-eyed.' On a visit to Papua New Guinea in 1998 he remarked to a British student who had trekked in the country: 'You managed not to get eaten then?', and to Aboriginal leader William Brin at the Aboriginal Cultural Park in Queensland, 2002, he asked: 'Do you still throw spears at each other?'

QUEEN ELIZABETH I

Queen Elizabeth I regarded herself as a paragon of cleanliness, declaring that she bathed once a month, 'whether she needed it or not'.

The Elizabethans considered baths to be a luxury, or to be taken as a health measure, not to be indulged in all that often. By the standards of the day, a monthly bath was very frequent. Most of her citizens would only bathe a few times a year.

Elizabeth I was so apprehensive about having her rotten teeth pulled out, that the Bishop of London had one of his own teeth extracted to show her how easy it was.

It's said that Elizabeth's teeth were bad because of her love of sugary foods. The removal of Her Majesty's teeth led to a great deal of frustration among her courtiers, who couldn't understand her commands due to the fact that she spoke very quickly and with her lips wrapped round her gums. After her teeth were removed, Elizabeth only appeared in public with her mouth padded with wads of cotton.

Elizabeth made it compulsory for anyone over the age of six to wear a hat on Sundays and holidays.

It was a measure introduced to protect the country's wool trade, as woollen caps were becoming unfashionable. With the exception of 'Maids, ladies, gentlewomen, noble personages, and every Lord, knight and gentleman of twenty marks land' all were expected to wear 'a cap of wool, thicked and dressed in England, made within this realm, and only dressed and finished by some of the trade of cappers, upon pain to forfeit for every day of not wearing 3s. 4d.'. The legislation was repealed in 1597 as unworkable.

Despite being a studious intellectual who'd happily spend three hours a day reading history books, Elizabeth I would frequently spit, swear and blaspheme.

Elizabeth I frequently swore – especially when angry – and was well known for her 'round, mouth-filling oaths'. Indeed Elizabeth's chief advisor William Cecil once removed a book from the Queen's sight that was presented to her by a Puritan, Mr Fuller, in which 'Her Gracious Majesty' was sharply criticised for such behaviour. Fuller writes: '. . .by Your Majesty's evil example and sufferance, the most part of your subjects do commonly swear and blaspheme'. When Elizabeth demanded to see the book, Cecil declared it 'lost'.

Elizabeth I is believed by many to have been a man in disguise – the infant Elizabeth having been replaced by the Duke of Richmond's son by Mary Howard.

According to the legend of 'The Bisley Boy', a 10-year-old Elizabeth was sent to Overcourt House in Bisley to escape the plague but was taken ill and died. To avoid the deadly wrath of her father Henry VIII, her hosts substituted the young Elizabeth with a boy, the son of the Duke of Richmond, who was himself the illegitimate son of Henry VIII so had similar looks and colouring. This, it is maintained, explains Queen Elizabeth's fondness for big dresses and high necklines, why she never married or had children, and why she left specific instructions for no post mortem to be carried out on her body after death.

QUEEN ELIZABETH II

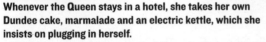

Whenever the Queen stays in a hotel, she takes her own Dundee cake, marmalade and an electric kettle, which she insists on plugging in herself.

Among the essential items packed for each trip are a kettle, a selection of teas and a stash of Dundee cake. She keeps her cornflakes in Tupperware containers, and listens to a Roberts radio in the morning while eating toast with a choice of marmalades, and doing the *Telegraph* crossword. Fond of familiar pleasures, the Queen stops every day at 5pm for a traditional English cup of tea.

The Queen is an excellent mimic and does surprisingly good impressions.

During her twenties, the Queen revealed herself to be a surprisingly good mimic, a talent she has kept to this day. Over the years, her favourite impressions have been Rolf Harris, René from *'Allo 'Allo* and Tony Benn, as well as the prime ministers she has known over the past half century.

Hanging her handbag over her arm is a signal to staff that the Queen is bored with the person she's talking to.

When the Queen hangs her handbag on her right arm at a public function it's a signal to staff that she's ready to move on. If she places her handbag on the table at a dinner it signifies she wishes the event to finish within the next five minutes. The Queen frequently has a handbag with her – even when 'off duty' in Buckingham Palace or her other residences – and desks and tables in most rooms are fitted with hooks for her to hang it on. She also carries an 'S'-shaped hook in her handbag to use if a pre-fitted one is not available.

Wherever she goes, the Queen takes an outfit in black in case she suddenly needs to mourn.

It's common practice amongst royal families. When the Queen's father died while she and Prince Philip were out in the wilds of Kenya, both had packed the requisite black outfits. When she received the news, the Queen and her husband were out animal-watching, and it's reported that the accompanying press pack stood on the road, with their cameras down at their sides to show they were respecting her privacy, and wouldn't take a picture until the royal party had returned to their luggage and put on their black outfits.

The Queen is known to her husband as 'sausage'.

The Duke of Edinburgh affectionately refers to the Queen by the pet names 'Sausage' and 'Cabbage'.

QUEEN VICTORIA

Queen Victoria eased the pain of her menstrual cramps by using marijuana.

She also used it for uterine bleeding, migraines, neuralgia and epileptic spasms. Her personal physician, Sir J. Russell Reynolds, prescribed her cannabis tincture, and wrote in an 1890 issue of *The Lancet* that: 'When pure and administered carefully, [cannabis] is one of the most valuable medicines we possess.'

Queen Victoria often put on a Scottish accent when travelling north of the border.

Victoria fell in love with Scotland and all things Scottish after her first visit in 1842, establishing tourism as a new Scottish industry.

Until the age of three Queen Victoria spoke only German.

As her father died when she was very young, Queen Victoria's early years were dominated by her overbearing German mother and her German governess Louisa Lehzen, from whom she only received a limited education.

Queen Victoria made it fashionable for brides to wear white.

Before Victoria selected a white dress, the bride would usually wear a coloured dress, and often simply wore her best gown for the wedding. At the time, Victoria's choice was criticised as she did not wear traditional royal trappings such as ermine, velvet trim or a crown, although the use of Honiton lace in her dress proved an important boost to the Devon lace making industry. Bizarrely, the wedding was reenacted in 1854 so that it could be captured by the new invention of photography.

Prince Albert was one of Victoria's closest male relatives.

Albert was her first cousin, and was actually born in the same year as Victoria, and even delivered by the same midwife. When he died aged 42, Queen Victoria wore black for the rest of her reign – nearly 40 years. Not even the wedding of her eldest son Prince Edward (later Edward VII) to Princess Alexandra of Denmark was sufficient to lift her spirits.

RABBITS

Spain literally means 'the land of rabbits'.

The name 'España' or 'Spain' derives from the Carthaginian word for rabbit, 'tsepan'. It is said that the Phoenicians and Carthaginians found the country overrun with these rodents, and so named it after them.

Beatrix Potter had her pet rabbit Peter killed with chloroform and then boiled its carcass to provide the model for Peter Rabbit.

Beatrix Potter, famous for writing and illustrating the Peter Rabbit children's books, also shot a squirrel out of a tree so she could study it as a model for Squirrel Nutkin, and chloroformed a bullfrog, then dissected it to help her create Jeremy Fisher. Historians say that Potter was a talented biologist who turned to writing children's books because 19th century scientists refused to take women researchers seriously.

During Bugs Bunny's long career, both the Broccoli Institute of America and the Utah Celery Company lobbied hard to get the rabbit to switch to their vegetables.

It was to no avail as carrots remained the cornerstone of the comic rabbit's routine. Although Mel Blanc, the voice of Bugs, would have approved an alternative choice as he was allergic to carrots. They caused his throat muscles to tighten so he couldn't speak.

In 1726, a woman from Surrey became famous after she claimed to have given birth to 20 rabbits.

Mary Tofts from Godalming even convinced her doctor that this was true. King George I heard and believed her story and sent down his own doctor, who was so convinced that she had indeed given birth to rabbits that he promised to obtain a pension for her. Tofts only finally admitted the story was a lie under threat of torture.

The Emperor Napoleon was once so unnerved on a rabbit shoot after hundreds of rabbits ran at him that he fled in fear to his carriage.

Napoleon had organised the 1807 hunting party to celebrate a landmark peace treaty. A sycophantic employee bought hundreds of rabbits to ensure that the imperial court had plenty to shoot at, but unfortunately the lackey had bought tame rabbits. When Napoleon approached them, the bunnies thought they were about to be fed and rushed at him, forcing him to retreat to his carriage. Napoleon also suffered from 'aelurophobia', the fear of cats, so a lot of small furry things running towards him must have struck him with terror.

RED

As every schoolboy knows, red is the third colour of the speculum, being a subtractive binary hue with a wavelength between 6 and 6.2 thousand micro-newtons and a frequency of 2.

In human colour psychology, Red is associated with cowardice, laziness, greed, envy and Thursday. In scientific laboratories, signs warning of hazards are usually bright red to denote danger.

Every creature on earth knows the difference between red and green, except for guide dogs for the blind who cannot tell a red light from a green one. They are trusted to direct their owners across the street purely because they are known to be extremely lucky.

It is recognised that red is the most attractive hair colour by far, and yet when a survey was carried out in 2008 it found 62 of the world's 100 richest men were married to brunettes, 22 to blondes, 16 to 'raven-haired' women, and none at all to a redhead.

The American comedian 'Red' Skelton got his nickname from his first name 'Redvers'. He later took to dyeing his hair red to match his name – despite warnings that it would be professional suicide!

Silent movie star Clara Bow had her hair dyed red to match the fur of her two Red Setters. It had no adverse effect on her film career however, as she appeared solely in black and white.

Although they never go grey or bald, redheads start out with less hair than anyone else. They have an average of 90,000 hairs compared to the 140,000 you have if you're blonde.

Compared to other coloured hair, red hair is notably sensitive. Many red-haired people dislike going to the hairdresser as much as going to the dentist, as they can actually feel the hairs being cut. This sensitivity isn't only restricted to hair; in fact research has shown that people with ginger hair require 20 per cent more anaesthetic before surgery than people with other coloured hair.

The spice ginger gets its name from the profuse red hairs found sprouting from the root before it is shaved for market.

Scientists in South Korea have manipulated the genes in a cat to make it glow red. The so-called 'Fire Cat' gives out enough light to read a book by. The scientists explain that they have done this to benefit the animal because the red cat will now be invisible to dogs. Meanwhile scientists in North Korea have been working on a project to make everyone in South Korea glow red in the dark.

FACT 🔴: Scientists in South Korea have manipulated the genes in a cat to make it glow red.

FACT 🔴: Research has shown that people with ginger hair require 20 per cent more anaesthetic before surgery than people with other coloured hair.

FACT 🔴: Redheads start out with less hair than anyone else. They have an average of 90,000 hairs compared to the 140,000 you have if you're blonde.

FACT 🔴: When a survey was carried out in 2008 it found 62 of the world's 100 richest men were married to brunettes, 22 to blondes, 16 to 'raven-haired' women, and none at all to a redhead.

FACT 🟢: Guide dogs for the blind cannot tell a red light from a green one.

SAUSAGES

In Britain, sausages are called 'bangers' because they used to explode.

During the Second World War, sausages contained so much water, as well as other items such as sawdust, that they exploded when they were fried as the heated water caused the skin to rip.

In parts of tropical Africa there is a tree known as the sausage tree, which has long fruits that look just like sausages.

The sausage-shaped fruit can grow to over a metre in length. Not everyone calls it the sausage tree; the Ashanti people of Ghana call it '*nufatene*' which means 'hanging breasts'. Perhaps unsurprisingly given its suggestive shape, the fruit has been used as an aphrodisiac, amongst other things. There is now a Sausage Tree pub in High Wycombe.

The world's longest sausage ever made was over 35 miles long.

It was made in Britain by J.J. Tranfield (on behalf of Asda) in October 2000 during British Sausage Week. The enormous sausage weighed 15.5 tonnes.

From 1939 to 1940, Finland and the Soviet Union engaged in the 'Sausage War'.

Otherwise known as The Winter War, the name came about after a starving Soviet battalion had performed a brilliantly executed night attack on an important Finnish supply position. However all started to unravel after the Soviet troops caught the scent of just-cooked sausages wafting from the Finnish mobile field kitchens (like those pictured), stopped their military action and began to stuff their faces. In the counter-attack, the Finns practically destroyed the whole Russian battalion. Many Russians died still chewing on their sausages.

In 2008, *Who Stole My Sausage* became the world's first canine theatre production.

The show took place at an arts festival in Glasgow, and featured sights, sounds and smells designed to capture the attention of dogs. Tickets were priced at £5 for dogs; humans went free.

SHEEP

The association between lamb and mint sauce in England was caused by Queen Elizabeth I's decree that lamb could only be eaten with bitter herbs.

Queen Elizabeth's bizarre decree was an attempt to discourage the consumption of lamb and mutton in order to maximise the availability of sheep for the declining wool industry. Mint sauce was the best response English cooks could come up with.

Black sheep are more likely to be struck by lightning than white sheep.

A thunderstorm in Lapleau in France in 1968 occurred, during which lightning struck a flock of sheep, killing all the black ones, but leaving the white ones untouched.

Scientists have created a self-shearing sheep.

A cross-breed sheep called Exlana is being developed by farmers in South West England, using imported semen from exotic breeds such as the Barbados Blackbelly and St Croix. The Exlana have shorter and more sparse hairs than other sheep, and moult their woolly coats in the field when spring arrives, saving farmers time and money. However, this does mean the sheep are liable to suffer from sunburn.

A cross between a sheep and a goat is called a 'geep'.

The geep is a sheep–goat chimera produced by fusing sheep and goat embryos. The result is an animal with a mixture of sheep and goat tissues, meaning that the parts that grow from the sheep are woolly, and those that grow from the goat are hairy.

In Montana it is illegal to have a sheep in the cab of your truck without a chaperone.

The use of 'the cab of your truck' makes clear the type of vehicle they expect likely offenders to have. Some other bizarre American motoring laws: in California, no vehicle without a driver may exceed 60 miles per hour; and in Oregon, a door on a car may not be left open 'longer than necessary'.

SHOES

The 'poulaine' was a 14th century shoe with a tip as long as two feet.

The length varied by social status: two feet for princes and noblemen, one foot for rich people of lower degree, and only half a foot for common people. Such shoes proved a hazard among the French crusaders at the Battle of Nicopolis in 1396 when they had to cut off the ends of their shoes in order to be able to run away.

The word 'sabotage' comes from the French word for a wooden shoe.

When workers' jobs were replaced by machines during the French industrial revolution, factory workers would throw their wooden shoes, or '*sabots*', into the machinery to wreck it, which is where we get the words 'saboteur' and 'sabotage'.

Prostitutes living in 16th century Venice wore shoes with heels that were so high that the courts eventually banned them.

These unfeasibly high-heeled shoes were called 'chopines' – the courtesans had to lean on sticks to walk in them. Venetian courts banned the shoes due to the many deaths caused by tripping and falling accidents.

Cinderella's slippers were originally made from squirrel fur.

Charles Perrault, who wrote the well-known version of the story in the 17th century, misheard the French word '*vair*' (meaning squirrel fur) in the medieval tale from which he took his updated work, and replaced it with the similar-sounding '*verre*' (glass).

A pair of shoes has been invented that vacuum as you walk.

These 'Shoovers' are officially called the 'Dustmate', and each sole has a tiny rechargeable vacuum in the base that collects dust as you walk around the house, which makers Electrolux claim is perfect for people with busy lifestyles.

SLEEP

In 1900, a normal night's sleep was nine hours.

Six to eight hours per day is the average amount of sleep a person needs. That's about one-third of a lifetime. As a population, we sleep about one to one-and-a-half hours less than we did 100 years ago.

Lee Hadwin of Henllan, North Wales, is a talented artist when he is asleep, but when awake he struggles to draw at all.

Lee is a sleepwalker, and draws all over the house at night, including on walls and tables, but cannot remember creating the drawings when he wakes up, nor can he recreate them. After filming his nocturnal activities, experts remain baffled, and the Edinburgh Sleep Clinic calls him 'unique'.

The earwig is so called because it was thought that they crawled into your ears when you were asleep.

When we used to sleep on pillows stuffed with straw, earwigs would crawl out and mistake ear holes for their natural hiding places.

Humans are the only animals to sleep on their backs.

According to Dr N.V. Nimbkar: 'The human species is the only obligatory bipedal animal and no other animal lies on its back for any length of time except in a temporary assumption of a supine position. Animals never sleep, lie or hibernate on their backs.'

Horses can sleep standing up.

They can do this due to their ability to lock their knee joints. As horses are prey animals, they prefer not to sleep on the ground, as this would make it more difficult to run away quickly if attacked. This is also the reason horses do most of their sleeping during the day. In fact, people are so unused to seeing horses lying down, that the police report they often get calls from members of the public who believe the relaxing horses to be dead.

SMOKING

Tobacco was originally smoked through the nose.

American Indians fashioned a special pipe with a forked end, designed to fit into the nostrils. The smoke was then inhaled through these ends by short, violent snorts. The name of this pipe was a tubak – and thus our word 'tobacco'.

Plague in 1665.

Smoking tobacco was once prescribed as an anti-plague remedy.

In Holland 'anti-plague pipes' were manufactured by the thousands, and during the plagues of 1665–66 and 1721, smoking was actually made compulsory at Eton public school.

In the early days of North American colonisation, smokers would sometimes add minced beavers' testicles to tobacco.

Beaver testicles were prized for their medicinal qualities and were regarded as both a natural pain killer and a contraceptive.

Today more than 600 items, from acacia gum to ylang ylang oil, are on the Department of Health's list of permitted additives to tobacco. The list includes castoreum extract, a product traditionally obtained from beavers' testicles.

A Tobacco Drinker, 1623

In 1997, Robert Brett left his entire fortune to his wife, provided she smoked four cigars a day for the rest of her life.

The Californian included this condition as his wife hadn't allowed him to smoke at home. This is just one of many bizarre edicts left in wills: in 1960 Samuel Bratt left his wife the sum of £330,000 on condition that she smoked five cigars a day; and the German poet Heinrich Heine left his estate to his wife on condition that she remarry so 'there will be at least one man to regret my death'.

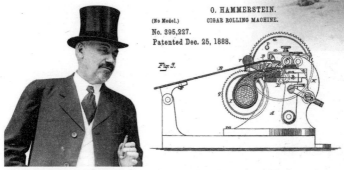

O. HAMMERSTEIN.
CIGAR ROLLING MACHINE.
(No Model.)
No. 395,227.
Patented Dec. 25, 1888.

Fig. 3.

The composer Oscar Hammerstein patented the first cigar-rolling machine in 1883.

Oscar Hammerstein was the grandfather of the lyricist Oscar Hammerstein II of Rogers & Hammerstein. His first job in New York as a young immigrant was sweeping in a cigar factory for three dollars a week, and he progressed in the trade quickly, leading to a job editing the US *Tobacco Journal*. However, Hammerstein's true passion was for the performing arts, and he used the proceeds from his cigar machines to bankroll opera productions and theatre building, and is credited with rekindling the popularity of opera in America.

SNOW

All snow crystals are hexagonal.

Although snowflakes can consist of ice crystals in all kinds of complex shapes, the crystals themselves all have six sides. This is because a snow crystal's shape reflects the internal order of its constituent water molecules; in a solid state, such as in ice and snow, water molecules form weak hydrogen bonds, and these ordered arrangements result in a symmetrical, hexagonal shape.

In 1876, a wealthy French woman left a large sum of money in her will to provide clothes for snowmen.

Madame de la Bresse, an eccentric and a prude, shocked her heirs by leaving 125,000 francs to properly clothe Parisian snowmen, for the sake of *'la décence'*. Her heirs claimed she was clearly mad and attempted to contest the will, but it was upheld by the presiding judge.

Children at a Norfolk school have been told not to throw snowballs unless they ask their target's permission first.

According to the *Daily Mail*, other members of the 'Snowball Taliban' include the North Wales Police, who instructed patrols to be on the look-out for snowball offenders after a youth was arrested for allegedly pelting a younger child with snowballs, breaking three teeth.

It has snowed in the Sahara Desert.

Snow is not that uncommon in the Sahara Desert. In recent memory it's snowed there in 1979, 2005, 2008, 2010 and 2012.

The world's tallest snowman was over 122 feet tall.

The world's tallest snowman – or snowwoman to be precise – was built by residents of Bethel, Maine, in the US over the period of a month and completed in February 2008. The snowwoman, named Olympia after Maine senator Olympia Snowe, was dressed in a 100-foot scarf, had 27-foot evergreen trees for arms, and eyelashes made from old skis.

SOAP

The French use almost half as much soap per head as we do in the UK.

The per capita use of soap in the UK is 40 ounces per year, whereas in France it's only 22.6 ounces per year. The American soap industry's journal describes the per capita use of soap in both France and Italy as 'exceedingly small'.

Because Arabs read from right to left, soap adverts showing clean laundry on the right, soapsuds in the middle and dirty stuff on the left, are a disaster there.

An advertising campaign in the 1970s displaying just such an image was a failure in Saudi Arabia. In Africa, packaging often shows an illustration of the contents of the food, due to poor literacy. This has meant that infant milk products showing pictures of babies have been similarly badly received.

The most expensive bar of soap in the world contains fat from Italian Prime Minister Silvio Berlusconi.

It was reported by the BBC in 2005 that a bar of soap made from excess fat taken from Italian Prime Minister Silvio Berlusconi had been sold for $18,000 (£9,862) by artist Gianna Motti. He bought the fat from a clinic where Mr Berlusconi had a liposuction operation performed.

Argentinean artist Nicola Constantino has made 100 soaps and two sculptures from her own fat.

She calls it 'savon de corps'. The fat was removed using liposuction. The artist also does her own interior decorating, and likes to show off her anus sofa in front of her wall of animal fetuses.

An American company has manufactured a soap that releases caffeine into the body, providing the same energising effect as two cups of coffee.

The soap is called 'Shower Shock', and is designed for busy people who do not have time for both a shower and a cup of coffee in the morning. However, the claim that caffeine can pass rapidly from the lather and be absorbed by the skin in any quantity remains unproven.

SOCKS

The Romans wore socks with sandals.

Roman legionnaires wore sock-type garments under their sandals in both Northern and Southern England, probably due to the cold climate. The earliest known surviving pair of socks, which date from 300-500 AD, were excavated from Oxyrhynchus on the Nile in Egypt and are on display in the V&A museum. They had split toes so they could be worn with sandals.

Both men and women are more likely to orgasm while wearing socks during sex.

In 2005, scientists at the University of Groningen found that, during tests, roughly 80 per cent of the sock-wearing couples were able to achieve orgasm compared with 50 per cent without. The scientists believe this is because the couples were more comfortable, and as such more relaxed, when they didn't have cold feet.

The Russian word for sock is pronounced 'nosock'.

It is spelt '*hocok*'.

The expression 'put a sock in it' dates from a time when woolly socks were often stuffed into gramophones to reduce the noise.

The phrase, meaning to be quiet, dates from the late 19th century, when early gramophones amplified sound through large horns and had no real volume control. It has also been suggested that it could have developed out of First World War military slang, meaning to stuff a sock in the mouth.

In the early 1700s, a French naturalist made socks from spiders' webs.

François Xavier Bon de Saint Hilaire boiled spider cocoons and extracted the silk threads to create socks, as well as gloves, stockings and reportedly even a suit for Louis XIV. Spider-silk weaving was once common in Madagascar.

SOUP

Despite cooking it for several days, Victorian eccentric Francis Buckland found that elephant trunk soup was still too chewy.

A founder member of the 'Society for the Acclimatisation of Animals in the United Kingdom', an organisation that believed exotic species should not merely be imported for display in zoos but should be domesticated and eaten, Buckland served many strange meals, such as mice on toast, roasted parrots and rhinoceros pie, and declared that the only things not edible were moles and bluebottles.

Alexander Graham Bell, inventor of the telephone, liked to drink his soup through a glass straw.

Bell used a thick glass straw to consume soup, and a thinner one for less viscous liquids. His wife Mabel considered them unsanitary as the straws were hard to clean.

In some rural parts of China, you can get owl soup.

According to Chinese folk remedies, owl soup was prescribed for headache, consumption and rheumatism. Those who have eaten it say it has the appearance of chicken soup, so the owl's head is usually retained as proof. In the US, efforts to list the spotted owl as an endangered species in the 1980s fuelled a heated battle between the federal government and the logging community. It created a wave of anti-spotted owl propaganda, including mocked-up cans of 'Cream of Spotted Owl' soup.

Some Amazonian tribes make a soup with the ground bones of their dead relatives.

The Yanomamo tribe use ground fragments of teeth and bones left after cremation, mixed with plantain soup, which is eaten by the closest living relative. In the Amahuaca tribe, soup is blown or vomited over youngsters at harvest time to make them strong.

At the end of every live performance, The First Viennese Vegetable Orchestra chop up their instruments and turn them into a soup which is shared with the audience.

This nine-member Austrian group plays instruments made out of fresh vegetables, including carrot flutes, eggplant drums, and a 'gurkaphone' which is a hollow cucumber with a carrot mouthpiece and green-pepper bell.

SPIDERS

All spiders are completely nocturnal, and thanks to their eight specially-adapted ears they are able to hear in the dark.

It's well known that spider silk is surprisingly weak and yet if a spider could spin a thread as thick as a pencil, it could stop a Boeing 747 in full flight.

Sexy underpants made from spider's web silk were a failure, as people found their flies kept getting caught in them.

Miss Muffet was the step-daughter of Dr Thomas Muffet, an entomologist who studied all manner of insects, including spiders. The well known nursery rhyme was in fact based on his scientific collaborator, Sir Charles Incey-Wincey.

In Borneo the Warawak Indians play a game similar to tennis using large tropical leaves as racquets and a live tarantula spider as the ball.

The tarantula has a lively bounce, especially on clay. Surprisingly few players are bitten, but the game is notoriously dangerous for the ball boys who have to pick up the angry spiders when they are knocked out of bounds.

If you were to cook a Venezuelan Goliath bird-eating tarantula you'd find the meat quite pleasant, tasting more like prawn than chicken, and what's more everybody gets a leg and you could also use the spider's fangs as toothpicks.

American cotton farmers welcome the arrival of the Summer Field spider among their crops as it feeds on the notorious boll weevils. This is why to this day it is against the law to tread on a spider in Alabama.

Among the specially adapted spiders, the Sprinter spider of the Serengeti is actually able to outrun a cheetah. Flying spiders have been known to make flights across the Mozambique Channel to Madagascar. Jumping spiders have been known to reach a height of 22,000 feet.

TV megastar James Corden is one of the few living people to have had a spider named after him. It's his nephew's pet spider, 'James'.

Harrison Ford, despite once being arachnophobic, has turned his California pony stables into a spider ranch. The US Natural History Museum has named a spider in his honour: 'Calponia Harrisonfordi'. Sadly the Harrison Ford spider was killed by a dung beetle rolling a huge ball of dung downhill and crushing him.

The first movie to feature the amazing Spiderman was made in 1943, with Clifton Webb in the starring role. Webb went on to star in several spin-offs.

FACT ☺ : If a spider could spin a thread as thick as a pencil, it could stop a Boeing 747 in full flight.

FACT ☺ : Miss Muffet was the step-daughter of Dr Thomas Muffet, an entomologist.

FACT ☺ : If you were to cook a Venezuelan Goliath bird-eating tarantula, you could use the spider's fangs as toothpicks.

FACT ☺ : Jumping spiders have been known to reach a height of 22,000 feet.

FACT ☺ : Harrison Ford has turned his California pony stables into a spider ranch. The US Natural History Museum has named a spider in his honour: 'Calponia Harrisonfordi'.

SUGAR

Before chemical tests were developed, doctors tested for diabetes by tasting a patient's urine.

Until the early 1800s, diabetes diagnosis was often made by 'water testers' who would taste the urine to detect sweetness. In Ancient India, doctors got round this problem by using ants, which would be attracted to the sweet-tasting urine.

In Boston, Massachusetts, 21 people were killed and eight buildings destroyed by a 15-foot high wave of sugar.

The Boston Molasses Disaster occurred in 1919, when a storage tank on Boston's waterfront burst, releasing two million gallons of molasses in a 160-foot wide wave that raced through the north of the city at 35 mph, causing $100 million worth of damage.

Motor manufacturer Henry Ford believed eating sugar was dangerous.
He feared the crystals would tear his stomach lining and cause internal bleeding. Henry Ford would also monitor his employees' social lives, and thought soya was a miracle food.

On a dry tongue, sugar has no taste.
This is because receptors on taste buds can only detect the chemicals from food once they've been dissolved by saliva.

Cats can't taste sugar.
Unlike other mammals, cats can't taste sweetness as they lack the genetic code to make the protein required for the tongue's sweet taste receptors. However, in other areas the cat has more sensitive tastes, such as detecting how long meat has been dead.

SWIMMING

Kangaroos are excellent swimmers, and have been found swimming as far as a mile off the Australian shore.

While kangaroos can only move their hind legs together on land, in the water they are able to kick each leg independently, and the animal has even been seen body surfing. However, swimming is not without danger for the animals, and in 2007 a kangaroo was mauled to death by a shark in the surf of Southern Australia. Wallabies are also strong swimmers, and have been known to swim from an island in Lake Wendouree, Victoria, to the mainland in order to nibble on people's gardens.

Swimmers in Rochester, Michigan, must have their bathing suits inspected by a police officer before swimming in public.

The US has strict rules about displays of nudity, as this Californian statute makes clear: 'Within the city, no person shall appear, bathe, sunbathe, walk or be in any public park, playground, beach or the waters adjacent thereto, in such a manner that the genitals, vulva, pubis, pubic symphysis, pubic hair, buttocks, natal cleft, perineum, anus, anal region, or pubic hair region of any such person, or any portion of the breast at or below the upper edge of the areola thereof, of any such female person, is exposed to public view or is not covered by an opaque covering.'

Tuna never stop swimming.

Tuna must swim constantly to get enough oxygen and stay alive. At an average speed of 9 mph, tuna swim up to 216 miles a day, 78,840 miles a year and 1,182,600 miles in a 15-year lifetime.

About 1,600 Belgians turned out to vote in their country's 2003 national elections wearing only swimming costumes or trunks.

This was the result of a promotion by Virgin Express, who had offered free flights to Bordeaux or Mallorca for the first 1,500 people who voted in their beachwear.

Writer Evelyn Waugh attempted to commit suicide by swimming out to sea, but turned back to shore after being stung by jellyfish.

The *Brideshead Revisited* author fell into a depression while teaching at a prep school in North Wales, and intended to commit suicide at sea, leaving behind his clothes and a scrap of paper on which he had written a few lines copied from Euripides about how the ocean washed away all human sorrows. After only a few yards he turned back after being stung on the shoulder by a jellyfish.

TAXIS

The word 'taxi' arrived with the invention of the 'taximeter' by Wilhelm Bruhn in 1891.
The taximeter measures the distance travelled and time taken for each journey, allowing an accurate fare to be charged. When taxis were first fitted with the modern taximeter, the cabbies of Stuttgart were so appalled at having their incomes regulated that they carried the inventor Wilhelm Bruhn through the streets and threw him in the river. The first reference to a 'taxi' in the UK was in 1907. Before that, they were known as hansom cabs or hackney carriages.

The name 'hackney carriage' came from the French word *'haquenée'*, meaning 'an ambling horse or mare'.
It has nothing to do with the London borough.

An early form of taximeter was used in ancient Rome.
Known as an 'odometer', it was a device fixed to the axle of a cart that released small wooden balls to denote the distance travelled. Roman author Vitruvius describes such a device, though the actual invention may have been by Archimedes.

In 1914 the French general Gallieni urgently needed to transport 6,000 troops from Paris to fight in the Battle of the Marne, so he sent them in a fleet of taxis.

With German forces close to achieving a breakthrough against beleaguered French forces outside Paris between 6–8 September 1914, emergency French troop reinforcements were sent on 7 September using a fleet of Parisian taxi cabs, some 600 in all, ferrying approximately 6,000 French reserve infantry troops to the front. The tactic worked and Paris was saved – just. The incident quickly gained legend as 'The taxis of the Marne'.

An 89-year-old woman disliked waiting in airports so much that she took a £2,000 taxi ride from the UK to Greece.

In 2007, Kathleen Searles made the 3,000-mile journey from Sussex to Mieza in three days, and insisted it was money well spent, even though she only spent four hours there. Taxi driver Julian Delefortrie said: 'When she asked me if I'd like to drive to Europe I replied that I would love to. I never expected her to say Greece!'

TEA

When tea was first introduced to America, housewives ignorant of its purpose served the tea leaves with butter after first throwing away the water in which they had been boiled.

Before tea gained popularity, the leaves were served like vegetables, or a form of porridge. In Ancient China, tea leaves were eaten as vegetables during spring and autumn, and some chefs today combine tea with spices to season chicken, steak and fish.

The tea bag was invented by mistake after a tea merchant gave his customers samples of his tea wrapped up in silk cloth; not certain how to open the bags of tea, they used them instead as tea bags.

New York tea salesman Thomas Sullivan shipped his tea bags around the world. The loose tea was intended to be removed from the sample bags by customers, but they found it easier to brew the tea with the tea still enclosed in the porous bags. So popular were these tea bags that they went to him for more. He was reportedly very surprised at his 'invention'.

The expression 'Cold Tea Syndrome' is one used in hospitals by medical staff to indicate that a patient has died.

It refers to the several cups of un-drunk cold tea on the deceased person's bedside cabinet. There are many other examples of medical slang: for example, a 'Hasselhoff' is a patient who gives doctors in A&E a bizarre explanation for their injury, after *Baywatch* actor David Hasselhoff said he'd hit his head on a chandelier whilst shaving.

Every year in Britain, almost 40 people are admitted to hospital for injuries involving tea cosies.

The figure varies year on year, but in 2001, 37 people were injured by tea cosies, 165 by placemats, and 5,945 by their own trousers. There is evidence that the number of tea cosy injuries in Britain are rising year on year.

A Zambian man was granted a divorce after explaining that he went with another woman after finding a frog in a cup of tea that his wife had made him.

28-year-old Andrew Nyoka, whose surname means 'snake' in English, divorced his wife in 2001 after the judge agreed that the marriage could not be saved.

TEETH

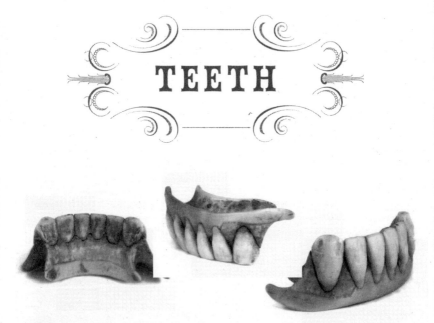

Early dentures were usually made with teeth pulled from the mouths of soldiers who had been killed in battle.

Before porcelain false teeth were perfected in the 19th century, the practice of tooth-robbing from corpses was common, as other available ivory teeth (hippopotamus, walrus or elephant) didn't look natural and deteriorated more quickly than human teeth. For many years after the Battle of Waterloo, dentures known as 'Waterloo teeth' were sold throughout Europe, consisting of teeth extracted from dead soldiers. As these soldiers were usually young men with good teeth, the dentures were prized for their quality, and some British wearers even considered it patriotic to sport the teeth of the vanquished foe.

False teeth used to be radioactive.

Old porcelain dentures often contained naturally occurring radiation in potassium-40, in addition to which manufacturers in the 1940s began to add uranium to the porcelain powder, believing that the fluorescence of the uranium helped to mimic the look of natural teeth. However, in addition to possible health problems, the uranium could also have the added disadvantage of fluorescing red, violet or bright yellow under UV lights.

A walrus 'walks' on its teeth.

Walruses use their tusks to help drag their bulky bodies out of the water and across ice floes, and the walrus's family name 'Odobenidae' comes from Greek, meaning 'one that walks with teeth'.

TEETH is an acronym used by doctors to mean 'Tried Everything Else, Try Homeopathy'.

Senior consultant Adam Fox from Guy's and St Thomas' hospital also revealed that: 'UBI' stands for 'Unexplained Beer Injury', an 'FLK' is a 'Funny Looking Kid', 'GPO' means 'Good For Parts Only' and 'GOK' means 'God Only Knows'.

Up until the 18th century, tooth decay was widely believed to be caused by a 'tooth worm'.

It was a widely held belief in Europe, even into the 20th century, that the tooth worm caused both toothache and tooth decay. This belief was probably due to the worm-like tubular structures found in teeth. In England it was thought the tooth worm looked like an eel, but in Germany the tooth worm or 'zahnwurm' was imagined to be a red, blue and grey maggot.

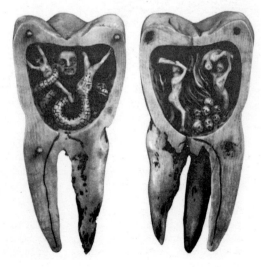

TELEPHONES

Today, Alexander Graham Bell is best remembered for inventing the bell, which was named after him. Telephones had been around for years, but before the bell was invented, nobody could tell when the phone was ringing.

When the first transcontinental telephone line was opened, the first words spoken by Alexander Graham Bell to his assistant 3,000 miles away in California were: 'Watson, please come here. I want you.'

The first telephones, mass produced by Henry Ford, made use of the new radio technology and could be carried around anywhere. However Edison devised a phone tethered by wire to the home to prevent theft.

Alexander Graham Bell made surprisingly little use of the telephone himself except for business purposes. He felt there was something improper about using the instrument socially, and in fact he never even phoned his wife or mother, preferring to send picture postcards or to call round in person.

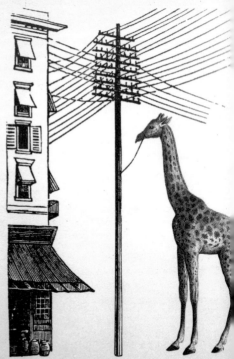

In London, when telephones first became popular, instead of having a Directory Enquiry service, callers would send a servant round to the home or office they were trying to contact to ask for their telephone number.

To this very day, if you call the California number Glendale 51510 you could get through to the late Amy Semple MacPherson. The American spiritualist and evangelist was buried with a live telephone in her coffin, although sadly she neglected to install an answering machine.

Mark Twain, who had no time for science and technology, stated that the telephone would never last – there was no need for it as people could already send messages quite easily with their fax machines.

Nowadays in the UK it's estimated there are five times as many phones as there are rats.

The single problem facing the early American phone networks was animal interference. In Nevada, columns of soldier ants would march up the poles and along the wires causing terrible interference on the line. Vibration on the ground was also a problem, and in California it is actually against the law for a circus parade including elephants to pass closer than 500 yards from a phone line. Browsing could also cause trouble, and in Atlanta, Georgia, it is illegal to tie a giraffe to a telephone pole.

The song 'Wichita Lineman' is wrongly thought to refer to a telephone company engineer, but is now more correctly known as 'Wichita Assistant Referee'.

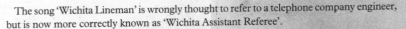

FACT ❶ : When the first transcontinental telephone line was opened, the first words spoken by Alexander Graham Bell to his assistant 3,000 miles away in California were: 'Watson, please come here. I want you.'

FACT ❷ : Bell never even phoned his wife or mother.

FACT ❸ : Amy Semple MacPherson, the American spiritualist and evangelist, was buried with a live telephone in her coffin.

FACT ❹ : People could already send messages quite easily with their fax machines.

FACT ❺ : In Atlanta, Georgia, it is illegal to tie a giraffe to a telephone pole.

TENNIS

Lawn tennis was originally played on an hour-glass shaped court.

Lawn tennis was first marketed as a game called Sphairistiké, a name taken from the Greek word '*sphairos*' meaning ball. It was patented by Major Walter Clopton Wingfield in 1874, in response to growing demand for gentle outdoor activities suitable for the middle classes, and sold over 1,000 sets in its first year, costing five guineas each. Wingfield's game was much as we know it today, except for the hour-glass court, which may have been adopted for patent reasons as it set his game apart from those using rectangular courts.

Notorious tennis 'grunter' Monica Seles is an anagram of 'Camel Noises'.

And Greg Rusedski is an anagram of 'Rugged Kisser'.

Zambian tennis player Lighton Ndefwayl blamed the loss of a match on lost concentration caused by his opponent farting when he served.

Ndefwayl also blamed his 1992 loss on the fact that his jockstrap was too tight, and said of his rival, Musumba Bwayla: 'Bwayla is a stupid man and a hopeless player. He has a huge nose and is cross-eyed. Girls hate him.'

Austrian Hans Redl played at Wimbledon for 10 years in a row despite losing an arm in the Second World War.

Redl played at Wimbledon from 1947 to 1956 after losing his left arm in combat. He managed to serve by tossing the ball up in the air with his racquet.

Tennis is the sport with the highest ratio of officials to participants.

There are 11 officials to two players, including a referee, a chair umpire, a line umpire and a chief umpire. The number of officials on court is necessary to make sure they can view every area of the court during the fast-paced game.

THE MOON

Although the moon looks round to us, it is in fact shaped like an egg.

Because the moon's pointed end faces towards the earth and it keeps the same face pointed towards us all the time, we are not aware of the moon being slightly egg-shaped.

When the Apollo 12 astronauts landed on the Moon in 1969, the surface vibrated for very nearly an hour.

Astronaut Pete Conrad is quoted on NASA's official website as saying: 'The entire moon rang like a gong, vibrating and resonating for almost an hour after the impact.' These vibrations have led geologists to theorise that the moon's surface is composed of fragile layers of rock.

In 1835, the *New York Sun* claimed that the eminent scientist Sir John Hershel had spotted furry winged men resembling bats on the surface of a full moon.

'The Great Moon Hoax' was perpetrated in a series of six articles by Richard Adams Locke, a Cambridge-educated reporter working for the *New York Sun*. As well as bat-like winged humanoids, his articles also claimed that the moon was populated with bison, goats, unicorns and tail-less beavers.

27 per cent of Americans believe we never landed on the moon.

Surveys have also found that over four million Americans believe they've been abducted by aliens.

The chances of being bitten by a dog are twice as high during a full moon.

The correlation between bites and full moons was discovered by the Bradford Royal Infirmary, which reviewed 1,621 cases of dog bites between 1997 and 1999.

THE POSTAL
SERVICE

BHUTAN

The Kingdom of Bhutan issued a stamp that was actually a small phonograph record which played the Bhutanese national anthem.

Bhutan have previously issued stamps made out of steel and silk as well as vinyl, and in 2008 they issued a CD-ROM stamp.

When Iraqi terrorist Khay Rahnajet didn't pay enough postage on a letter bomb he'd posted, it came back with 'return to sender' stamped on it.

Forgetting it was the bomb, he opened it and died in the explosion. Rahnajet was nominated for a Darwin Award in 2000. These awards are named in honour of Charles Darwin, and commemorate those who improve our gene pool by removing themselves from it.

In 1920 the US Postal Service declared it would no longer allow children to be sent by post.

With the advent of Parcel Post in the US in 1913, several children were sent in the post, the logic being that, if they weighed less than 50 pounds, it was considerably cheaper than paying a standard rail fare. In 1918 seven-year-old Josephine McCall and eight-year-old Iris Carter were delivered by parcel post from their home in Red Top to their aunt in Springfield. It cost $1.23 to send them both and the children were stamped like ordinary parcels.

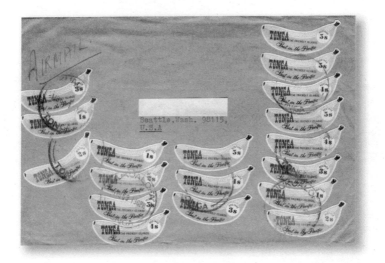

Tonga once issued a stamp in the shape of a banana.

The 1969 stamp was worth 1 seniti.

Author Anthony Trollope is credited with introducing the post box to Britain.

Anthony Trollope's report of postal services on the Channel Islands recommended the introduction of pillar boxes, resulting in the first rectangular green boxes appearing in Britain in 1854. These boxes allowed people the luxury of private correspondence, although it was not until 1874 that they were first painted their now-familiar red. Trollope worked for the Post Office for 33 years, during which time he also wrote 48 novels, waking at 5.30 am to write a thousand words before heading to work.

TIGERS

All tigers share similar markings on their forehead, which resemble the Chinese symbol Wang, meaning 'King'.

The Chinese character ' 王 ' means 'king' or 'emperor', and its similarity to the tiger's marking has resulted in tigers being seen as the king of all animals in Chinese culture.

Tiger whiskers can be fatal.

In 16th- and 17th century Sumatra and Bali, a common method of revenge, particularly against cheating husbands, was to place finely chopped tiger's whiskers in your enemies' food. Tiger whiskers were even cited in Marie Vassiltchikov's 'Berlin Diaries' as a potential method of assassinating Hitler. It was believed that the numerous whisker barbs would get caught in the victim's digestive tract, causing sores and infections. However, in India and Pakistan, tiger whiskers are prized as a medicine to aid childbirth.

In India and Bangladesh, people wear facemasks on the backs of their heads to prevent tiger attacks.

Tigers usually attack from the rear, and so the masks provide protection by confusing the cats into seeing another face. Since the people of the Sundarbans started wearing the masks in 1986, tiger attacks have been almost eliminated, although it is now thought that they are decreasing in effectiveness as the tigers learn the trick.

Unlike most cats, tigers love the water.

While most cats avoid water as they are adapted to hunt on land, tigers must cross rivers in their jungle habitats in order to chase prey. Tigers can easily swim three or four miles in one go, and a tiger might swim up to 18 miles per day in the course of patrolling its territory.

Tigers have striped skin as well as striped fur.

If you shaved a tiger, you would still be able to see its distinctive pattern on its skin. In contrast, polar bears have black skin, and translucent hairs; it is the light reflecting off them that makes them look white.

TOILETS

Before the invention of toilet paper, people used to use a mussel shell called a scraper.
In desert regions, sand was often used, in the American South, corncobs, and the
Romans used a vinegar-soaked stick with a sponge on the end.

91 per cent of British women won't sit properly on public toilets.

A survey of 30,000 British women found that most prefer to adopt a semi-squatting position over the toilet instead.

The proposed Westminster & Chelsea Hospital was renamed after officials realised that the initials would be WC.

Officials realised the potentially embarrassing acronym just in time, and the name was changed to the current Chelsea & Westminster hospital just before the Queen came to officially open it.

The average person spends three years of their life on the toilet.

People visit the toilet an average of 2,500 times a year, the equivalent of six to eight times a day, and women spend longer on the toilet than men.

The new Wembley stadium has more toilets than any other building in the world.

The stadium, which has a circumference of one kilometre, is proud to boast 2,600 toilets and could hold seven billion pints of milk.

TOMATOES

The world's largest tomato plant covers an area the size of an Olympic swimming pool.
The plant can be seen at the Epcot greenhouse at Walt Disney World Resort in Lake Buena Vista, Florida, USA, and measures over 610 square feet.

Tomatoes contain nicotine.

A tomato contains a small amount of nicotine, although the levels decrease as it ripens. Even so, some programmes to help people quit smoking recommend giving up tomatoes in order to eliminate low-level nicotine intake. Other foods that contain nicotine include aubergines, cauliflowers and potatoes. 10 kilos of aubergine have the same nicotine content as a single cigarette.

In the year 2000, food manufacturer Heinz produced tomato ketchups that were green, blue, orange, purple, pink and teal.

They were made by adding food colouring to Heinz's traditional ketchup. In the first three years Heinz sold more than 25 million bottles of their coloured ketchup but consumers eventually lost interest and the product was discontinued in 2006.

Heinz Tomato Ketchup has a speed limit.

According to Heinz's own website: 'ketchup exits the iconic glass bottle at 0.028 mph. However, if it pours unaided at more than 0.028 mph, it's rejected for sale'.

Even though our gastric juices are acidic enough to dissolve metal, we cannot digest tomato seeds.

Tomato seeds pass straight through our intestines due to 'endozoochory'. Many plants that have brightly coloured and succulent fruits, such as grapes, plums and raspberries, have indigestible gelatinous coats that allow the seeds to pass through an animal undamaged. This is necessary as the parent plants rely on animal consumption and dispersal in droppings for reproduction.

TRAINS

A cat has been appointed a stationmaster in Japan.

Dressed in a railwayman's cap, the cat is named Tama, and welcomes passengers at the unmanned Kishi station on the Wakayama electric railway. The appointment has proved incredibly popular, drawing tourists and generating revenue for the Wakayama electric railway.

When travelling by train, Lord Berners used a large clinical thermometer to take his temperature rectally every five minutes until his train compartment was clear.

The composer and renowned eccentric was also known to beckon passengers into his compartment by waving out of the train window while wearing a black skull cap and black glasses.

The longest station platform bench in the world is in Scarborough.
It measures 456 feet and can seat 228 passengers at any one time.

At the start of the railways there were public fears that high speeds would cause mental disorders in passengers.
Dr Dionysus Lardner, Professor of Natural Philosophy and Astronomy at University College, London, thought that the rapid movement would cause brain deterioration, and that those looking at moving trains would suffer from vertigo. Lardner also believed that passengers travelling at high speed would be 'unable to breathe' and would die of asphyxia. As a result, railway pioneer George Stephenson was forced to allay fears by reporting to MPs that trains would never go faster than 12 mph.

The longest ever train was 7.353 km long.
The BHP Iron Ore train consisted of 682 ore cars, pushed by eight diesel-electric locomotives. In 2001, the train travelled 275 km from the company's Newman and Yandi mines to Port Hedland, Western Australia.

TROUSERS

The reason that trousers are referred to in the plural is that they were for several centuries made in two parts, one for each leg.

Before modern tailoring, the pieces were put on each leg separately and then wrapped and tied or belted at the waist, and the plural usage has continued out of habit, even though construction techniques have changed. This is the same for all similar garments, such as breeches, shorts, tights and knickers. In contrast, a shirt has always been one piece of cloth, and so is singular.

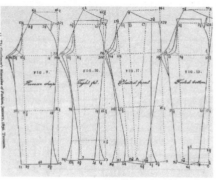

Viscount Evan Tredegar trained his parrot to climb up inside his trousers and peep out through the fly.

The eccentric aristocrat encouraged the parrot, called Blue Boy, to perform the trick to break the ice at parties. The outlandish Welsh poet was Queen Mary's 'favourite bohemian', and also known as an accomplished occultist, building a 'magik room' at Tredegar House.

In New Zealand in the 1930s, farmers had trouble with exploding trousers.

Farmer Richard Buckley noted a string of detonations in his trousers as he hung them out to dry in front of a fire in 1931, but many less fortunate farmers were wearing their trousers when they went off. This phenomenon was the result of using sodium chlorate as a weed killer to remove problematic ragwort, a chemical which unfortunately becomes violently explosive when combined with organic fibres, such as cotton or wool.

Whenever the opera composer Puccini invited attractive women to dinner, his wife soaked his trousers in camphor.

Elvira Puccini was obsessively jealous of her husband's numerous infidelities, which he referred to as 'cultivating little gardens', and she was also known to put bromide in his coffee after such dinners. On one occasion, when an attractive singer called to the house on a professional matter, she was threatened by Elvira with an umbrella, and chased out.

In an average year in Britain, trousers cause twice as many accidents as chainsaws.

In some years the figure can even be higher; in 2001, the Department of Trade and Industry reported that 5,945 people were hospitalised by trouser-related accidents, as opposed to 1,207 relating to chainsaws.

UMBRELLAS

The introduction of the umbrella angered London cabbies.

When Jonas Hanway brought the umbrella back from Persia in the 1750s, London cabmen and sedan-chair men saw it as a threat to their business as London's rain showers were a prime source of trade. English gentlemen often referred to their umbrellas as a 'Hanway', although, curiously, Hanway's memorial plaque in Westminster Abbey honours his commitment to prostitutes, but makes no mention of his groundbreaking service to the rain umbrella.

In 1786, Barbeu Dubourg of France invented a 'lightning-conductor umbrella'.

The physician, botanist, writer and translator was a keen follower of the work of Benjamin Franklin. Dubourg's invention consisted of an umbrella fitted with a tall spike and trailing chain, which was designed to give gentlemen the same protection offered to women in fashionable lightning-conductor hats.

In 1903, Pierre Vigny, a French master-at-arms, established a self-defence academy in London with his wife, and together they gave lessons in the use of umbrellas and parasols as defensive weapons.

It was not the first use of the umbrella in this way. In 1838, Baron Charles de Berenger suggested methods for using the umbrella as a defence against highwaymen and ruffians. More recently, one of Nicolas Sarkozy's bodyguards would carry a £10,000 Kevlar reinforced umbrella to protect him from thrown missiles. The umbrella had been successfully tested against attack dogs, knives, acid and thrown projectiles.

In China, a woman blown off a six-storey building landed safely because her umbrella slowed her fall.

In 2007, Zhang Haijing fell from a roof in Zhejiang Province after airing some clothes during a storm. Doctors believe her life was saved by the umbrella she was carrying, although she did suffer from fractured chest bones after landing in a vegetable garden.

The world's only Umbrella Cover Museum is on Peak's Island in the US state of Maine.

The museum's curator is Nancy 3 Hoffman, who changed her middle name to '3' after a typing error. The 612 umbrella covers on exhibit come from more than 30 countries, and a guided tour includes Nancy 3 Hoffman singing 'Let a Smile Be Your Umbrella', accompanied by an accordion.

URINE

Laplanders drink urine to derive hallucinogenic effects.

Laplanders consume a mushroom known as 'fly agaric' and will often urinate into a pot so that their friends can then drink the urine and experience the same hallucinogenic effects. And there is evidence that Laplanders have given the mushroom to their reindeer to eat and then have drunk the reindeer urine. Some believe the myth of Santa's flying reindeer derives from this practice – the effect of fly agaric is similar to LSD.

The Romans bought bottled Portuguese urine to use as a mouthwash and to whiten teeth.

Portuguese urine was preferred as it was considered more potent. The practice became so popular that Emperor Nero put a tax on the collection of urine from Rome's great sewer. The Romans even sold urine from men's public urinals as a commodity; fullers would empty the urinal pots and use the ammonia-rich urine for laundering and bleaching togas and tunics. In fact, urine remained one of the most effective ingredients in mouthwashes until the 18th century. And in modern day India bottled cow's urine is sold as a medicine to be drunk as a health cure for ailments ranging from liver disease to obesity and even cancer.

Pee-odorant

During the Second World War the American government instructed pilots in the Pacific to eat asparagus so that any pilot who found himself stranded could simply urinate into the sea, and wait for the strong chemicals from the asparagus to attract fish.

In fact 'normal' human urine can attract fish on its own, and it is believed to be particularly attractive to saltwater bass. Human saliva is attractive to catfish. The 'smelly' urine induced by eating asparagus is not detectable by everyone: 90 per cent of the Israeli population are unable to smell it, as are 75 per cent of the Chinese population.

The ostrich is the only bird able to urinate.

According to *Black's Veterinary Dictionary*, the ostrich is the only bird known to pass urine; other birds combine solid and liquid waste in their cloaca.

Cat urine glows in the dark.

The colour depends on the age of the urine; fresh cat urine glows green, while dried cat urine glows yellow. If you have a cat and want to play this at home, it's easily done by purchasing a cat urine cleaner, which comes with a 'stain detective' black light: simply darken the room and watch the stains glow.

THE VIKINGS

Viking Leif Ericsson reached America from Greenland nearly five centuries before Christopher Columbus.

The Norse Sagas tell us that the Vikings settled in Newfoundland, which they called Vineland, sometime around AD 1000. This is supported by archeological evidence, which has found Norse-looking buildings from that date, along with iron nails, bone needles, bronze pins and yarn spindles.

Viking Eric the Red chose the name he did for Greenland as a simple marketing exercise to persuade his countrymen to settle there under the mistaken belief that the land was green and fertile.

Eric the Red discovered the country in AD 982 during three years of exile, and was so keen for people to settle there that he named it Greenland, when in truth it was not remotely green. His sales pitch is recorded in *The Saga of Eric the Red* as having been particularly successful with those living on poor farmland, and those suffering after a recent famine.

The ancient Vikings navigated at sea using ravens.

Viking sailors took on board a number of the birds, and released them one by one as they sailed to the west. If the raven flew back along the course the ship had already travelled, the sailors continued due west. But when a raven

flew in a different direction, the ships would change course and follow its flight path, hoping it would lead them to land.

The fearless Vikings would often head into battle without armour or even shirts.

As a result, our word 'berserk' is derived from the Norse for 'bare shirt'. The Berserkers were troops specially chosen for their hot-headedness, and would be whipped up into a pre-battle fury by their

leaders. They fought stripped to the waist or in skins, and were known to drink ale before a fight.

Ice-skating was first practised by Vikings in Sweden over 1,200 years ago.

The first primitive skates were made from the leg bones of reindeer or oxen, which were filed down to make a smooth surface and tied to the feet using leather straps. To this day, the Dutch word for skate is *schenkel*, meaning leg bone.

WALT DISNEY

In 1939, Walt Disney was presented with one full-sized Oscar and seven miniature Oscars for his classic *Snow White and the Seven Dwarfs*.

The awards were presented by a 10-year-old Shirley Temple in recognition of the surprise success of the film, which had previously been referred to as 'Disney's Folly'. Before release, even his own wife had said 'no one's ever going to pay a dime to see a dwarf picture'.

Among the names considered for the dwarfs in *Snow White* were Deafy, Dirty, Awful, Blabby, Burpy, Gabby, Puffy, Stuffy, Nifty, Tubby, Biggo Ego, Flabby, Jaunty, Baldy, Lazy, Dizzy, Cranky and Chesty.

Disney wanted the names to reflect characters, and in his notes for 'Awful' he writes 'He steals and drinks and is very dirty.'

The spacing between bins in Disneyland was determined by Walt Disney himself counting how many steps it took him to eat a hot dog and throw away the wrapper.

The result was about 20 steps, which is the distance used in every Disney park today.

In 1940, the FBI recruited Disney as an Official Informant. He was later designated Special Agent in Charge.

Disney was active within the FBI during the Second World War and the Cold War. When Disney testified as a friendly witness before the House Committee on Un-American Activities in 1947, he accused the League of Women Voters of being a communist organisation and the Screen Actors Guild of being a communist front.

According to the employee manual, Walt Disney would have been forbidden to work at any of his own theme parks because of his moustache.

Moustaches and beards were not allowed due to their communist connotations. Today you can work at a Disney theme park and sport a moustache, but you will have had to grow your moustache in your holidays. Beards, goatees and sideburns are still not permitted. Walt Disney himself grew his famous moustache at the age of 25.

WALTER RALEIGH

Sir Walter Raleigh famously had a third nipple and he also had six fingers on each foot.

Raleigh's ships were noted for the health of their crews because at the start of each voyage Sir Walter would give each crewman a basket of doughnuts and a small cask of Boots multi-vitamin pills. The sailors would give Raleigh three rousing cheers as they set sail and he waved them off from the dockside. Being a nervous sailor, Raleigh never personally visited Virginia or any other part of North America.

At Court, Raleigh devised a new kind of gavotte, where the dancers actually made physical body contact, known as 'Sir Walter's Gavotte'. It was later shortened to 'Walt's Dance' and further shortened to 'Waltz'. It was then banned as too lascivious and likely to spread crabs.

It's now believed to be highly unlikely that potatoes were introduced to England by Sir Walter Raleigh. He would have been far too busy running his bicycle factory.

Raleigh was furious when his captain returned from the Americas

with a cargo of useless leaves. He calmed down a bit when Sir Francis Drake showed Raleigh how to smoke the tobacco using a clay pipe. Raleigh found he much preferred it to the electric cigarette he'd been accustomed to.

Although it was Lord Burleigh who actually invented the bicycle, it was first manufactured by Raleigh's factory which bore his name: 'Walter's Wheels'. As a publicity stunt he organised major cycling events and 'bicycle rallies' bear his name to this day.

Raleigh's luck ran out when he was falsely convicted of stealing a loaf of bread from the Earl of Sandwich, for which in those days the penalty was death.

Raleigh spent 15 years on death row writing his projected five-volume 'History of the World', though he never got further than 1300 BC.

During his time in prison, Queen Elizabeth would visit him every single day. She often smuggled in a sweet trolley hidden under her voluminous skirts.

After Raleigh's execution, his head was embalmed and presented to his wife. She carried it with her at all times in a velvet bag until she died. She was much in demand at Halloween parties.

In the town of Raleigh, South Dakota, smoking tobacco is banned except on 28 September which commemorates Potato Day. Potato Day was born in Raleigh and she grew up to be an overweight but popular burlesque dancer.

FACT ●: After Raleigh's execution, his head was embalmed and presented to his wife. She carried it with her at all times in a velvet bag until she died.

FACT ○: Raleigh spent 15 years on death row writing his projected five-volume 'History of the World', though he never got further than 1300 BC.

FACT ●: Sir Francis Drake showed Raleigh how to smoke the tobacco using a clay pipe.

FACT ○: It's now believed to be highly unlikely that potatoes were introduced to England by Sir Walter Raleigh.

FACT ●: Raleigh never personally visited Virginia or any other part of North America.

WASPS

The Potter wasp makes its nest out of clay and in the shape of a vase.

Also known as the Mason wasp, these solitary insects will then hang their egg inside on a dried thread and stock the vase-shaped nest with a paralysed caterpillar, spider or beetle larvae on which their single larva will feed when hatched. In contrast to their young, the adult wasp feeds on floral nectar.

A type of Australian wasp has the scientific name 'Aha ha'.

The 'Aha ha' was named by entomologist Arnold Menke in 1977, as when he opened the package containing the specimen, he exclaimed 'Aha!' Menke also used the wasp's name as his car number plate. Other insects have been given equally ridiculous names, including an arachnid

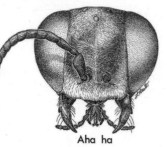

Aha ha

called 'oops', a colonid beetle called 'colon rectum', a rhinoceros beetle named 'enema pan', and horseflies named 'gressittia titsadasyi' and 'tabanus rhizonshine'.

Entomologist Justin O. Schmidt has created a 'sting index' ranking the painfulness of various different wasp stings from his own experience.

THE UNBELIEVABLE TRUTH

The 'Schmidt Sting Pain Index' ranks the stings of 78 species, including wasps, bees and ants, on a scale of 1 to 4 and describes the stings in fantastic detail, with certain distinctive creatures acting as benchmarks. At the low end of the scale the sweat bee is described as '1.0: Light, ephemeral, almost fruity. A tiny spark has singed a single hair on your arm', whereas the bullet ant, rating 4.0+, has a sting that is 'Pure, intense, brilliant pain. Like fire-walking over flaming charcoal with a 3-inch rusty nail in your heel.'

In 1981, experts involved with the Dangerous Animals Act agreed that an animal was officially dangerous if its sting was 'worse than two wasps'.

Other qualifications cited were if its scratch or bite was worse than a domestic cat, or its kick harder than a billy goat or horse.

Wasps can be trained to sniff out drugs or explosives.

Biologist Felix Waeckers has found that wasps are quick learners and more effective than dogs at finding substances like marijuana and explosives, with the Brecon wasp taking less than an hour to train. When the wasps smell substances, they move their heads in a feeding motion, which can be picked up by electronic sensors. A team from the University of Georgia has developed a handheld chemical drug detector powered by five wasps, nicknamed 'the wasp hound'.

5 The software measures the dark spots around the pin hole against the white back-ground of the cylinder cap.

1 Scent Chamber

2 Web camera

4

3 Fan

5 The software graphs the degree of crowding around the pin hole and determines if this is the smell being sought. The result is usually out in 30 seconds.

WIGS

In the 18th century, men and women wore very tall, white-powdered wigs called macaronis.

The bigger the wig, the richer and more important the person.

Between 1701 and 1708, the Governor of New York, Lord Cornbury, wore a powdered ladies' wig.

Lord Cornbury, the third Earl of Clarendon and a cousin of Queen Anne, was a transvestite who made his entrance at the New York Assembly wearing a blue silk gown, a head-dress studded with diamonds, a ladies' fan and satin shoes. The heavily built man spent a fortune on women's clothes for himself, and even received hand-me-downs from Queen Anne.

Robert Hawker, a 19th century vicar, liked to wear a wig made of seaweed and pretend to be a mermaid.

The churchman liked to sit on a rock off the coast at Bude, wearing only a wig of seaweed and an oilskin wrapped around his legs. This was a hoax played on the superstitious people of Bude, many of whom thought he was a real mermaid.

Kate Winslet used a pubic wig, or merkin, in the film *The Reader*.

Winslet found it difficult to grow sufficient extra pubic hair for the film role, due to years of diligent waxing. Merkins are usually used in Hollywood films to prevent accidental genital exposure during nude scenes.

In Tokyo, they sell wigs for dogs.

Many Tokyo dog owners have several dozen different outfits for their dogs. Japan's famous New Year Dog Party, which attracts up to 40,000 visitors, features activities such as dog yoga and dog fashion shows.

WINDOWS

According to the Bible, Noah's Ark had one window.

In the King James Bible, Genesis Chapter 6:16 contains these instructions for building the ark: 'A window shalt thou make to the ark, and in a cubit shalt thou finish it above.' However, there is debate about whether this means a single window, 18 inches square, which would be impractical for a vessel full of thousands of animals, or a ventilating window that would run around the vessel at the height of a cubit. Dutchman Johan Huibers chose the latter interpretation for his full-scale, functioning model of the ark, based on the Bible's instructions.

Patients with windows in their hospital rooms recover more quickly.

In 1984, environmental psychologist Roger Ulrich found that patients recovering from gallbladder surgery who had bedside windows looking onto leafy trees healed, on average, a day faster, needed significantly less pain medication, and had fewer postsurgical complications compared to those with views of a brick wall.

TV and radio presenter Dermot O'Leary kisses a window every night.

Dermot revealed this superstitious practice in an interview with *The Guardian*, stating that he doesn't know why he does this, but never forgets to do so 'even when I'm drunk'.

In 1994, Los Angeles police arrested a man for dressing as the grim reaper and standing outside the windows of old people's homes, staring in.

The prankster – complete with hooded black cloak and scythe – was known as the 'Grim Peeper'.

According to the British Trust for Ornithology, in the UK up to 100 million birds crash into windows each year, with a third of them dying as a result.

To reduce fatalities the BTO suggests people put stickers shaped like birds of prey in their garden windows.

WOLFGANG
AMADEUS MOZART

Mozart's full name was Johann Chrysostomus Wolfgang Gottlieb Mozart.

'Amadeus' is Latin for Gottlieb and means 'God's Love'. Other memorable middle names include Richard Tiffany Gere and Harry S. Truman, where the 'S' stands for nothing, despite the full stop.

Mozart composed a clarinet trio entirely in his head while he was out bowling.

Mozart's trio for clarinet, viola and piano was nicknamed 'The Klegelstatt Trio', *klegelstatt* being the Austrian term for 'bowling alley'. It got its name as Mozart was supposed to have composed the entire work on a single day while out bowling with friends.

Mozart had a deformity of his left ear, which he kept covered with an ear-wig.

Doctors now refer to such similarly strangely shaped ears as a case of 'Mozart's ear'. The condition results in a bulging deformity to the exterior or 'pinna' of the ear.

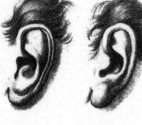

Mozarts Ohr. *Gewöhnliches Ohr.*

Mozart composed a piece that required the player to use his two hands and his nose.

Mozart challenged his friend Joseph Haydn to sight-read this composition in exchange for champagne. When Haydn declared the piece impossible to play (as it requires the right hand to be playing upper octaves, the left hand lower octaves, and a note in the middle to be struck simultaneously), Mozart showed him it could be done by using the player's nose. Haydn responded by saying, 'with a nose like yours, it becomes easier'.

Mozart wrote a canon in B-flat major called 'Leck Mich im Arsch' or 'Lick My Arse'.

With lyrics in German, it was one of a set of at least six canons probably written in Vienna in 1782. Sung by six voices as a three-part round, it was thought to be a party piece for his friends.

2. „Leck mich im Arsch"
(„Laßt froh uns sein")
Sechstimmiger Kanon
KV 231 (382c)

WOOL

'Doctor Who' Tom Baker's famous scarf was much longer than originally planned, because the knitter thought she had to use all the wool provided.

The designer gave knitter Begonia Pope a selection of balls of coloured wool to choose from, but she assumed she had to use them all, and knitted a scarf around 20 feet long. The scarf now has its own website.

The nursery rhyme 'Baa Baa Black Sheep' is thought to have been written as a protest against a wool export tax in 1275.

The wool industry was critical to the country's economy from the Middle Ages to the 19th century, and the song is thought to refer to Edward I's tax on wool exports from every port in the country. 'One for the master' refers to the tax payable to the king, 'one for the dame' was the local landowner, and 'one for the little boy' was the producer.

Wool was once commonly used as an early form of toilet paper.

Wool was used by wealthy Romans and Vikings, as well as the French and British later on.

In Victorian Britain, it was believed that woollen underwear possessed miraculous health benefits.

This 'Wool Movement' began under German naturalist and hygienist Dr. Gustav Jäger, a former professor of physiology at Stuttgart University and inspiration for the foundation of the Jaeger clothing brand. Dr Jäger advocated the health benefits of wearing coarse, porous and un-dyed wool in contact with the skin, as the fabric allowed the body to breathe, unlike – he maintained – any kind of plant fibre. His advocates included Oscar Wilde and George Bernard Shaw.

In 1770, parliament rejected a bill banning women from using wool to seduce men.

Some women went to such lengths in the pursuit of extravagant 18th century fashions, that the proposed act was to 'protect men from being beguiled into marriage by false adornments [. . .] by the scents, paints, cosmetic washes, artificial teeth, false hair, Spanish wool, iron stays, hoops, high-heeled shoes and bolstered hips'. The bill also proposed that women found guilty of this should face the punishment for witchcraft. Spanish wool was noted for its high quality, and before the 18th century, the export of Merinos from Spain was a crime punishable by death.

Published by Windmill Books 2014

2 4 6 8 10 9 7 5 3 1

First published in Great Britain in 2013 by Preface Publishing

Windmill Books
The Random House Group Limited
20 Vauxhall Bridge Road, London SW1V 2SA

Addresses for companies within The Random House Group Limited can be found at:
www.randomhouse.co.uk/offices.htm

The Random House Group Limited Reg. No. 954009

www.randomhouse.co.uk

A CIP catalogue record for this book
is available from the British Library

ISBN 9780099559139

Typeset by Tony Lyons and Neal Townsend

Printed and bound by Clays Ltd, St Ives PLC

MIX
Paper from
responsible sources
FSC
www.fsc.org
FSC® C018179

Penguin Random House is committed to a sustainable
future for our business, our readers and our planet.
This book is made from Forest Stewardship
Council® certified paper.